Overthinking

How to Stop Worrying, Reduce Your Anxiety, Eliminate Negative Thinking and Use Positive Energy to Control Your Thoughts and Make Better Decisions in Your Life

Author

Ryan Creed

accurate, up-to-date and reliable complete information. No warranties of any kind are expressed or implied. Furthermore, the author is not engaged in the rendering of legal, financial, medical or professional advice.

By reading this disclaimer, the reader agrees that under no circumstances are we responsible for any losses, direct or indirect, which are incurred as a result of the use of the information contained within this document, including, but not limited to: errors, omissions, or inaccuracies.

TABLE OF CONTENTS

Introduction

Do You Overthink Everything?

Nothing in this world can trouble you as much as your thoughts.

Overthinking is a concept that many of us today are all too familiar with. However, there are many conflicting opinions on this subject. Some say that it's healthy for personal growth; others say that it is a bad habit and can negatively affect one's general well-being. But hold on for a minute — if someone asks you if overthinking is terrible, what would you say?

You might be influenced by these conflicting opinions and the many preconceived ideas that you might have developed as a result of what you have heard, read about, or experienced. I hope that my detailed research, coupled with the real-life experiences neatly outlined in this book, will help you to clarify some of your questions and concerns. So I will give you some time to reflect on my research and experiences; you will be able to confidently answer that question by the time you are done reading.

You may have sometimes asked: Does he or she think about me? Did I forget to lock the door? Why did I say that stupid thing? What will I tell my boss tomorrow? Yes, we do not only ask these questions, but we also overthink them. These questions drive us crazy — even when we want to stop thinking about them, it seems that there is no way out!

But why exactly do we overthink? Well, let's first take time to appreciate how amazing and incredible it is to think about the future or possible scenarios — things that will or might happen. Yes! It's indeed a gift. But can this gift be wrongly used? Think about a knife; it serves a valuable purpose, but if improperly handled, can it be used disastrously? We both know the answer. You see, just like a knife, this beautiful gift — the ability to think — can be wrongly used too.

If we always worry, plan, and try to predict what the future will hold, our anxiety level will rise, frustration will be unavoidable, and stress will constantly knock us down. And yet we must think — that's what distinguishes us from animals, and that's why we can plan well, consider the relative possibilities of future events (usually based on past experience), analyze problems and thus, solve them.

Due to their capacity to think, many fortunate individuals have been able to invest, create, and learn more about the world around them. This incredible benefit can prove harmful as well. So, many questions arise. How might we achieve a balance between overthinking and not thinking enough? Is it possible to stop overthinking and then relax one's mind? We can start our quest by considering what facts support the argument that overthinking is wrong, bad, or negative.

Before I explain vividly all that this book is designed to capture, let's examine how the brain functions, as that will serve as a foundation for what you will be reading in the subsequent chapters.

The brain, as revealed by science, is an intricate part of the human body. The reptilian brain, as the oldest part of the brain, is what is responsible for the primary functions we engage in. These functions involve body temperature, breathing, balance, and heart rate. And these functions in our body system are what we have no awareness of; however, in the background, they are routinely happening.

The other part, the prefrontal cortex, is responsible for complex thinking that encompasses abstract thoughts, decision-making, and inhibitory control. These behaviors, in humans, are what help us to take in the information around us, reflect carefully, make our decisions, and plan for the future.

However, when you continually beat yourself up due to the mistakes you made in the past or worry about whether you will succeed in the future, you end up feeling anxious and worried, emotional states that render you less capable of making logical, sound, balanced decisions. Rumination does not assist us with problem-solving.

Now, let's highlight this book's features, which will help you to develop a clearer understanding of what overthinking is and what you need to know about it. Designed to help you understand the principles of overthinking, the first part of the book explains what makes overthinking problematic; it describes how you can focus less on outcomes. Limiting your thinking to the original purpose it was created for, the benefits of meditation, avoiding perfectionism, and how to get the best out of overthinking are extensively discussed. The next chapter will help you to see if you've been gripped by overthinking, as it explains what overthinkers do but would never talk about.

Chapter Three highlights practical steps (starting with the restoration process) to help you stop overthinking, tells you what you should stop thinking about, describes how to prevent yourself from denying what you are thinking about, and gives you some practical tips that will help you to do away with overthinking completely.

The fourth chapter aims to capture the types of thinking that exist — positive and negative. And it goes to explain the effects of both positive and negative thinking. Further to the restoration process, Chapter Five explains quick tips and practical ways to attain good energy that will reinforce your conviction to discard overthinking.

The sixth chapter addresses worry and the best ways to cope with it; it answers a few common questions that people have regarding worry and provides a detailed answer to them. Though anxiety is difficult to quit, this chapter provides some out-of-the-box solutions. The concept of basic mindfulness meditation isn't adequately understood today. Thus, many do not know how to go about it; after reading Chapter Seven, you will be equipped with the best tips and tricks to go about it.

How do you further strengthen your desire to stop overthinking? I'll take you by the hand in Chapter Eight to reveal the best training strategies for stress reduction and curbing anxiety, the facts regarding anxiety and excessive worrying, and some basic ways to solve those symptoms.

In the ninth chapter, you will master how to quickly embrace mindfulness and utilize it for replacing overthinking — a tool to assist your prefrontal cortex. In conclusion, the tenth chapter will outline clear ways to make better life decisions, how not to fear decision-making. Conclusively, in the final chapter, I've compiled things that aren't worth thinking over.

As a bonus, I have included overthinking checklists at the end of this book. As an everyday guide, use these lists to go about your day-to-day activities.

Happy reading!

Chapter 1

Understanding the Principles of Overthinking

True freedom is achieved when we free ourselves from the prison of our false thoughts.

One common problem that many people encounter while trying to achieve their dreams is overthinking. Yes! It can help us greatly to chase our wildest dreams, but it comes with huge disadvantages.

What Makes Overthinking a Big Problem?

One bad thing about overthinking is that one can easily become addicted to this way of life. Many have seen this as an opportunity to distract themselves from the reality of daily life. Undoubtedly, we could and do face a variety of different problems each day, but focusing more on these potential problems will mean that we are disconnected from the present moment.

When you dig deep into yourself, you can achieve more; you can surpass limits and accomplish many things. But if you overthink excessively, you will end up hurting yourself. You will also keep doing things that are not healthy for your body. However, if you can resist the urge to overthink, you have a much greater chance of achieving happiness.

Your day-to-day tasks can only be accomplished when you are in good health. The best way to achieve this is to engage some form of daily exercise; most individuals who seek good health fit in some form of workout every day. As they attain a higher level of health, they become better equipped to overcome emotional blocks and to develop patterns of clear thinking.

How can you also overcome emotional blocks that may limit your success? How can you feel more joy, unite your mind, body, and soul, and become more productive in your daily activities? Reading further will allow you to explore the answers to these questions.

The rules that I will discuss will help you become more self-confident. You will come to value yourself more, and this will help you to live the life you were created to live. Only then will you be able to find satisfaction in life.

In life, to accomplish any goal, it can be extremely helpful to have a set of rules or guidelines to follow — here are some that will help you break free from overthinking.

Focus Less on Outcomes

Whatever activity you are involved in, you should have a clearly defined goal. This will provide you with a starting point that will help to determine the correct direction or course of action that you should take, a way to measure your progress and success, and an incentive to improve and grow. Having a goal that you feel motivated to achieve will inspire you to lead a happy, healthy, fulfilling life.

But achieving goals first involves identifying and accepting the present condition we are in. Hard as it may be to accept an unpleasant reality, that is the first step to addressing the issue at hand.

Are you overweight? You need to accept the fact today if you want to shed some weight tomorrow. However, you should love yourself as you are, even if you're trying to make changes to your look. That love will help you to direct your energy into activities, people, places and situations that will help you improve your one and only body. Understanding this truth will eventually help you to find complete relief from your daily worries.

Start by looking back at your past. Resist the urge to regret any decisions you have made to improve your life, even if the outcomes were not what you hoped for. Instead of focusing on things that did not go as planned, why not focus on the accomplishments you have achieved over the years; this will help you achieve even more in the future. Focusing on past negative outcomes will not help you achieve positive future ones.

Take a Daily Dose of Meditation

You need to learn more about yourself every day; one of the best ways to achieve this is through meditation. You can greatly improve your mental and emotional health if you take time each day for yourself and use that valuable quiet time to meditate.

Meditation will help you to clear your mind so that you can better focus on who you are and what you truly want in life; it is one of the best ways you can develop a clear insight into your life. This insight will make it easier for you to stay true to yourself. Furthermore, it will help you to identify any problems you are facing and seek the guidance needed to break free from these problems.

With what result? You can start to put your heart and soul into working on creative ideas that will help you to improve your life and to achieve your goals.

Avoid Being Paralyzed by Perfectionism

Who says that you must be a perfectionist to be successful in life? It will only make it more difficult for you to reach your goals. For example, a perfectionistic person trying to lose weight might become so careful about what he/she eats, how he/she trains, etc. that he/she might lose sight of his/her real goals.

You don't need to be perfect to reach your goals; you only need to keep putting in the necessary effort to achieve success. What does this involve? Cultivate virtues like patience. Trust your abilities and be consistent. If you take the perfectionistic route, you will always find something you're not doing right each day; you will be focusing negatively on what you don't want. This will not help you to achieve positive outcomes.

Instead of striving for perfection, address each day as they come, work hard, and focus positively on achieving your goals. In the long run, you will achieve what you set out to do, but, in the meantime, keep finding ways to improve, to be just a little bit today than you were yesterday.

Don't Dwell on What Others Think About You

The truth is, people can be so critical. Despite your efforts, some people will never appreciate anything you do or achieve. Negative, critical feedback may make you feel scared or less confident; you may feel as if you are not anywhere close to success. Overcoming such feelings can be extremely difficult.

It is impossible to know exactly what others are thinking. Remember, everyone may see a different version of you, depending on what they choose to look at and the cognitive biases that they possess. Often, how they perceive you may not have anything to do with who you really are. Also, their opinions may change, depending on a multitude of different factors.

So, difficult as it often is, you need to try to worry less about what others think about you. If people find what you are doing interesting, that's great! If they don't, it is not a reflection on you and how interesting you really are. You need to be able develop an opinion of yourself that is independent of what others think of you, and this is something that many people struggle with.

Many won't care about what we do; everyone has a right to determine their own priorities, goals, wants, and needs. You deserve to have a life that is appealing by your own standards, not just society's.

Break Big Goals Into Smaller Ones (Daily, Weekly, Monthly, and Yearly)

Your goal is huge, and that's great! But what does it include? The best way to know is by having an outline, a detailed plan to achieving your dream. Instead of chasing it all at once, why not break it into smaller, manageable goals? This will allow you to enjoy the journey towards achieving your big goal or dream.

Breaking larger goals down into smaller ones will help you stay motivated. You will face tough times, but you can overcome them if you remind yourself of the smaller successes you have achieved on the way to your larger ones. Enjoying these positive outcomes will contribute to your momentum along the way to your greatness!

Tips

Attaching a deadline to a goal is a good thing; it will help you work harder and achieve your goals more quickly. But be flexible; along the way, you may need to adjust your methods or strategy. Just because you don't meet this self-imposed deadline doesn't mean that you will never achieve your dream, and you need to give yourself enough space to reevaluate your timeline if necessary.

Getting the Best Out of Overthinking

Overthinking is not something new to HSPs (highly sensitive people) and Introverts; it is something they are good at doing. Overthinking is one of their specialties.

When faced with any situation, they sit and think extensively about the situation. They critically analyze each situation just to ensure they get the best results. An introvert won't stop thinking. It is their way of life; they will never stop.

For example, someone who enjoys a good creative writing class may tend to always overthink. The best way to build the best scenario, to develop the role of each character, and make a story come alive is by thinking deeply about the story and carefully considering all of the different scenarios which could occur.

Unfortunately, most overthinkers do it the wrong way.

They spend too much of their time trying to anticipate everything that could go wrong in their lives. Some worry excessively about what others say to them, analyzing their tone of voice and their expressions while relentlessly wondering if all of these signals mean that others are upset and angry at them.

Overthinking Can Be a Good Thing. Why?

There are situations where overthinking can be extremely valuable. Decision-making is one situation where introverts and HSPs make excellent use of overthinking. They carefully explore all their available options and attempt to view events from a variety of different perspectives. Normally, most people prefer to think things through before they make any type of decision.

In these situations, there is a greater chance of making the right decision when all options are considered carefully and a much lower chance of saying or doing things that will be later regretted. Weighing all of our different options before making decisions helps to reduce the possible risk associated with each decision.

However, when overthinking becomes excessive, it can be detrimental. At that point, focusing on only one course of action may prove difficult, as one who is overwhelmed by an abundance of options may feel compelled to consider all possible details or scenarios, including unlikely or irrelevant ones.

At this point, the most important thing is to search for ways to curb overthinking and clear the mind. That way, you can harness the power of overthinking and make it work for you rather than against you.

Using Overthinking to Your Advantage

Do you think you are good at overthinking? Are you scared it will impact your life negatively? Worry not; overthinking can be advantageous. The fact that you can easily think things through and analyze a variety of options is something that you can use to your advantage; you can consider situations from multiple angles in order to see each situation in a different light.

However, focusing solely on the negative aspects of your situation will prevent you from seeing solutions to your problems and could result in a downward spiral of negative thinking. This is when we start asking questions like: What if this is the wrong decision? Will I regret this in the future?

Visualize positively; that is when overthinking will start to work for you. All you need to do is ensure that your thoughts are channeled exclusively towards taking advantage of the positive aspects of the situation.

For example, sometimes, when we interact with other people, we start asking ourselves negative questions like: Was she angry about what I said when she saw me? Was he upset by my attitude? We need to choose our thoughts carefully and instead ask ourselves questions like: Is it possible that she was having a bad day, and her anger had nothing to do with me? Is it possible that he might have been upset by other things that might have been going on at home?

Are you taking full advantage of your overthinking superpower? You can do so by asking yourself some of the following questions:

- Am I sure of this, or am I just assuming?
- Is it likely that positive things will eventually happen to me?

- Was that person's reaction to me more about them than about me?
- What if events unfold just the way I want them to unfold?
- What if only the best-case scenario occurs?

Overthinking can easily go too far when we become overwhelmed by the abundance of options and preoccupied with the possibility of negative outcomes. Therefore, it's good to build up some resistance to this negativity spiral. Instead of focusing only on our negative thoughts and expectations and the negative possibilities, it is best to focus on the positive ones. The truth is, looking at the positive side of the story won't always be easy. But if you keep striving to do this, you'll start to make progress in no time.

Chapter 2

How to Identify If You Are an Overthinker

The biggest cause of unhappiness is overthinking.

A big gap exists between deliberating and solving problems. Some often suggest that women are more likely to overthink than men, but the truth is that no one manages to avoid overthinking; it is something everyone does.

A therapist meets with thousands of individuals in their office daily, many of whom are searching for help in dealing with overthinking. Many often complain about their inability to relax. They feel that their brain is constantly preoccupied with worries and negative thoughts, and, as a result, they feel so much anxiety that they can't rest. Some complain about the fact that they focus excessively on how much better their lives would be without the mistakes they have made.

There is a strong connection between overthinking and mental health problems, such as anxiety and depression. Those suffering from overthinking might not even notice the decline in their mental health because they are so preoccupied and worried; they are not living in the mindfully. Such individuals might feel that their overthinking is healthy and useful, and without it some horrible calamity might happen.

But the truth is just the opposite. Overthinking increases the chances of feeling lost, anxious, and miserable. It can also lead to resentment and anger that clouds your judgment and makes it hard for you to make the right decisions. This state is often referred to as analysis paralysis.

Forms of Overthinking

Overthinking keeps reminding you of things you can't control, such as your failure. There are basically two forms of overthinking, namely: an excessive rumination on the past and worrying excessively about future events. These preoccupations prevent you from making progress in your life. There is a clear difference between overthinking, self-reflection, and problem-solving.

How is overthinking different from problem-solving? There is a clear difference between problem-solving and overthinking. When problem-solving, your goal is to solve an underlying problem. Overthinkers dwell more on the problems themselves than possible solutions to their problems.

How about self-reflection? Is it the same as overthinking? No! Self-reflection has a definite purpose; it helps you discover new things about yourself, your condition, and your situation.

What's the bottom line? While you are overthinking, you're not productive. However, self-reflection and problem-solving help you create solutions and recognize behaviors that may be holding you back.

Are You an Overthinker?

We all have a tendency to overthink. Being aware of this fact makes it easier to change. And the first step involves identifying the damage caused by overthinking.

The idea that overthinking stops bad things from happening is a subconscious perception nurtured by many; they feel that the failure to ruminate over past events will precipitate some sort of unforeseen calamity. Research indicates that overthinking is not healthy and will impact our lives negatively.

Ten Signs That You Are an Overthinker

Consider the following signs that show you're overthinking:

1. You repeatedly mentally revisit embarrassing moments in your head.
2. You find it difficult to sleep because your brain just won't shut off.
3. You ask yourself numerous questions, such as: What if?

4. You spend time thinking about the hidden meanings in events and social interactions.
5. You repeat past conversations you have had with others and think about things that you should or shouldn't have said.
6. You always remember your mistakes.
7. You keep playing a script of what someone did or said that you're angry about.
8. You lose track of current events happening around you because you're lost in deep thought about the future.
9. You spend time worrying about things you have little or no control over.
10. You can't rid your mind of your worries.

If you notice the tendency to become enmeshed in overthinking, don't despair. You can use the strategies below to get back your energy, time, and brainpower.

From proper time scheduling to thought substitution, here are several exercises that will boost your mental strength and help you stop overthinking everything.

Things Overthinkers Do (That They Never Talk About)

If you are an overthinker, you limit your chances of becoming successful in life. It will prevent you from reaching your goals and make your life miserable.

Below are ten of the things overthinkers do without paying attention to.

They apologize excessively.

When you tell an overthinker that they have wronged you, before even identifying if the situation is their fault, they start to apologize. This leaves them exposed to additional criticism, which may or may not be warranted.

It is good to accept blame and reduce others' tension sometimes, but if this is done exclusively to please others, or because you're scared of what they will think about you, it is unhealthy.

An overthinker always wants to smooth things over with other people. This causes them more pain in the long run.

Critical thinking is their thing.

Most overthinkers are excellent critical thinkers. This is one of the excellent things about overthinking. An overthinker spends all of their time deliberating and analyzing each decision in an unending manner. Therefore, they often come up with the best results.

Overthinkers can punch their way out of a paper bag, but only after analyzing the entire makeup of the bag, and the soft spots. That takes a whole lot of time, but they deliver the best results. Often, overthinkers use their tunnel vision to focus relentlessly on a problem until they come up with a solution.

Sleeping is an issue.

An overthinker's brain never stops working. It keeps spinning at maximum speed all day long. This makes them restless, and sleeping becomes impossible. Their minds refuse to shut down, even when their body needs sleep.

They worry excessively about making others happy.

Overthinkers forget that they should be happy too. They worry about others' happiness, forgetting they need to be happy. They often negatively exaggerate how the world will view their feelings, actions, thoughts, decisions, and words.

This limits their progress and makes accomplishing their personal goals harder. They make decisions that please others, instead of themselves.

Overthinkers May Also Be Escape Artists.

In order to escape their own minds, overthinkers might resort to overworking, excessive activity, perfectionism, and other extreme habits to escape from their overthinking.

Those with more serious issues may turn to state-altering medications or drugs to take the edge off.

They experience severe headaches or migraines.

Catastrophic overthinking may cause somatization, such as headaches, stomachaches, etc. Those especially prone to worrying or overthinking may fear that their headache is a symptom of something more serious, which may make their headache even worse.

They research their purchases excessively or always need a second opinion.

When making purchases, those that overthink may become paralyzed with the overabundance of options that are available to them. They may search online for hours for the best options. They may ask all of their friends' opinions.

When shopping, they may need to consider multiple options or ask a friend to come along just to approve their choice. This comes from a place of low self-confidence. They wait for others to decide or approve what they will eat, wear, and do.

Their overthinking stems from insecurity.

They often overthink because they are unsure of their decisions; this makes it hard for them to decide on what to do. At work, they might have issues choosing clients, projects, or the best course of action to take when problems arise. This lack of confidence can lead them to be doubted by others, even when they end up making the right decisions.

They may become overly preoccupied.

They may not be able to see the forest for the trees. When they become overly preoccupied, they may miss important dates or appointments.

They may search endlessly for reasons to stop overthinking.

Some often admit that they overthink; it may be something that they always try to break free from. They may overthink about ways to stop overthinking.

19 Things You Need to Stop Overthinking

Sound, critical thinking is essential; however, overthinking can negatively impact your life, as I've described in the previous chapter.

Specifically, while there are a lot of things that people overthink about, there are some aspects of life that a person shouldn't even waste his or her time thinking about.

Let's check them out one by one.

1. Whether You Love or You Don't Love Someone

That shouldn't be rocket science. Because, finally, you either do or do not. For sure, whether you love the person or not, you will eventually know.

2. If the One Who You Love is The One You Will Want Forever

There is no genuine or sincere timeline; the only timeline is the stereotype that society portrays today. When you don't follow it, it might make you feel ashamed. For a lifelong decision, you don't have to be sure right away; many people aren't sure right away, either.

3. Mundane Social Discrepancies

You fear that people do not want to talk with/to you; as a result, you worry or think they don't want to hang out with you. No, that isn't necessarily the case. Sometimes, people don't have the time. So, don't panic automatically. The only time it means something is when someone says to your face that they aren't into you.

4. How You Appear to Others

How people view you depends on the filter that they view you through. This includes their own biases and beliefs about others. What they think and feel about you will seem accurate to them, but it might not reflect the real you. Know yourself and be positive.

5. The Difference Between What Someone Says and What They Mean

People don't always mean what they say! It can sometimes be easy for you to identify when they aren't entirely honest with you. Yes, it's a gut feeling; their body language speaks volumes. However, sometimes people will not be honest with you, and you will have to take them at their word, or not at all.

6.   The Grand Scheme of Things

Have you ever thought about how grand the whole world is? At a point, do you feel like proceeding? Certainly not! The vastness and mightiness of the universe, on the other hand, is awe-inspiring, and spending time to understand the details is an interesting but unproductive use of our imaginations.

7.   Your Exact Place in the World

Don't compare yourself to anyone. Where you are right now is your place. If you want to change, your subsequent destination is your new place. When it comes to where one needs to be in life, there is no right and wrong answer.

8.   Whether You Are Happy or Not

When you are overthinking about whether you are happy or not, you are not satisfied. Do you feel you delighted? If answering that is tough, then you are not happy.

9.   Whether You Have Made a Bad Decision or Not

If you keep dwelling on past choices, you will not change anything in your future. The right thing to think about is the step that you should take next.

10. Whether You Should Meet Up with Someone and Hang Out

You have many assumptions in your head: Will they say no, yes, or maybe? Will they reject you outright? Chances are they don't know what's in your mind. So, what's healthy here is give it a try. They might feel flattered and happy that you want to spend time with them and strengthen the relationship.

11. Every Minute Detail About Why Some Things Didn't Work Out

The moment has passed! You will not get the chance to work these things out now. So, let them go! For the sake of growth, you could reflect on those occasions, so you don't make the same mistakes again. However, when you overthink them, you will bury yourself in sadness and remorse.

12. How Society Will Define You

Society's labels don't define you. They are simply what people use to identify you. You do not have to use them to identify yourself.

13. Jokes

Sadly, many people overthink an excellent joke and become upset. They should just try to enjoy it. Overthinking jokes saps your joy. So, don't worry about what's behind everything that some people say.

14. Higher Spiritual and Deeper Philosophical Meanings Behind everything.

Most times, we don't need to know. And you will never know for sure, unfortunately.

15. Writing an Email

You should not re-read emails excessively before sending them. Imagine spending hours wondering if your email would make sense. Should you write it this way? I'm not saying one shouldn't think about this at all, but you should only spend a few moments composing and fine-tuning your message. So, while you need to be conscious of your words, don't overthink to the point that you will have to discard the idea of sending the mail entirely.

16. What Your Social Media Presence Reveals About You

I'm impressed by people who do not usually post pictures of their success and achievements on social media. It tells me that they are out there, living their lives and enjoying them, and that they are not sidetracked with what goes on around them. Also, it shows they immersed in the process of achieving their goals.

17. How Your Old Self Would See You

At certain stages in life, we have moments where we sit and ask ourselves how our younger self would see us. We could think thoughts like: How would I, five years ago, feel about me right now? He would be so disappointed in me. Well, forget about the old you for now; you're past that for a reason. The current you made certain decisions for a reason as well; respect them and respect your current self.

18. Your Output at Work

You may not always get complimented for a job well done. Most times, you just have to do your best and let everything else fall into place. You won't get any better at what you do by trying to get every colleague's opinion about your activities; it will just drive you crazy.

19.   Whether or Not to Talk to a Loved One

It's much quicker to simply just send a text or pick up the phone and call them.

Chapter 3

Practical Tips to Prevent Yourself from Overthinking

Let it go! Don't ruin a new day with overthinking about the previous day

We will see together in this chapter how to stop overthinking!

Overthinking is a bad habit that can often prevent you from taking action in life. On the contrary, you must work to reduce overthinking so that you can become more action-oriented!

If you learn how to stop overthinking, you have more free time to take on more projects. By doing this, you will seize more opportunities, and you will increase your chances of succeeding in your life!

When you overthink, it's often a sign that your ego prevents you from taking action due to a fear of failure! Did you know that failure helps you to learn what you need to know in order to improve and become a better person? This is a valuable lesson which will help you to improve your life.

How to Overcome Overthinking

Are you ready to conquer overthinking? In this section, there are 14 actions that you can incorporate them into your way of life to overcome this challenge of overthinking.

- Are you ready for changes?
- Are you ready to take some risks?
- Are you ready to discover the person behind the mask of stress?

Naturally, I would advise you to do these exercises step by step. However, if you prefer to do them in your own order, go for it. Do all the steps; you will be amazed at the results that you achieve.

Following all these steps will be essential for your success.

Recognize That You Are Worried

Believe me; many people refuse to recognize their own worries. They want to appear healthy, and by not admitting that they are anxious, they sink deeper into their stress. (I refused for years to recognize that I had a problem).

What kind of worry do you face?

- Is your worry based on something concrete? For example: Rumors circulating around your company announced that there would be layoffs, and all your coworkers are worried and stressed. But, has the company run into difficulties, or is it an unfounded rumor?
- You suffer from constant stomach cramps. You are afraid to get the results of your tests, and you are afraid that you may have an ulcer.

Or

- Is it the stress of anticipation? Well, every time you get stressed, does your sentence resemble one of the following sentences?
- If I miss my driver's license exam...

- If I tell my husband that...
- If I go for my radios and discover...

Whenever you plan your future, do you imagine harmful events or actions?

Identify the fear behind this stress

Fear of not being up to scratch, afraid of others' eyes, fear of illness, fear of being alone, fear of not having enough money, fear of being judged, abandoned, rejected, afraid of being humiliated, fear that we make fun of you, afraid to assert themselves, etc.

Honestly recognize what anguishes you:

- I'm afraid of losing my job, not finding others and finding myself without money.
- Yes, I tell my wife that I do not want to go to the X's, I'm afraid she'll cancel dinner with my CEO.
- If I fail out of university, I'm worried my parents will deprive me of holidays with my friends.
- If I tell Veronica that I'm not going to the movies, she'll get angry.

Verbalizing fear is a liberating act that allows overcoming long-term stress.

"The best way to eradicate fear is to confront it."
(Aboriginal proverb)

Once the fear is identified, ask yourself: Is it a REAL or IMAGINARY fear?

In other words, is it a fear that is based on something concrete, or is it an anticipatory fear?

Many people wonder how to stop worrying needlessly.

- Will your wife cancel dinner with your CEO if you refuse to go to the event next Tuesday?
- Will your parents take away your vacation with your friends if you fail out of university?
- Will Veronica get angry if you cancel your movie release?

"I'm an old man, and I had a lot of worries, but most never existed." - (Mark Twain)

Consider the worst risk or the event that might happen to you if your fear materializes.

- If I ask for a divorce, maybe I will only see my children every 15 days since my wife has already threatened me.
- If my boss dismisses me, will I find another job?

Be very honest with yourself; really go to the end of what you dread happening.

Are you ready to accept the risk of the worst-case scenario?

- "If I ask for a divorce, am I ready to see my children only every 15 days?"
- "If my boss tells me to look for another job, am I ready to be unemployed? "
- If the doctor tells me that I have cancer, what will I do?

"Accept what happens. This is the first step towards controlling the consequences of misfortune." - William James

Once the worst-case scenario and its risks are accepted, what actions can I take to find solutions?

- No, there is no reason for me to see my children only every 15 days, and I will fight for shared custody.
- If my boss tells me to look for another job, no problem. I have set my priorities, and I'm sure I'll find another job.
- If the doctor tells me that I have cancer, I will fight it, and if others have healed, why not me?

Ask yourself: What can I learn from this experience? What is my share of responsibility in what happens to me?

- Well, if I fail out of university, my parents can deprive me of holidays. But could I indeed have worked a little more?
- It will not be easy to fight this awful disease, but there were indeed a lot of things that were wrong in my life. I will start by taking care of myself.

Master your thoughts. Be positive!

Your life is a reflection of your thoughts. If you only think about illness, do not be surprised if you develop one. When you spend your time in perpetual fear of running out of money, do not be surprised to be continuously forced to count your pennies. If you are afraid of being fired, do not be surprised if your boss dismisses you.

- Surround yourself with optimistic and happy people.
- Avoid gossip like the plague.
- Only repeat positive things about your colleagues.
- Do not lend a compliant ear to all the rumors that circulate at your office or in your group of friends.
- As soon as you catch yourself worrying, immediately connect yourself to your most beautiful memory. See, feel and hear this wonderful memory.
- Be able to laugh at yourself.
- Take stock of what you have rather than highlighting what you are missing.
- Live one day at a time; it's easier.

- Go step by step and congratulate yourself on your progress every day.
- Watch funny movies.

Find a passion.

Learn computer science, gardening, astrology, knitting, and/or photography. Develop a passion for something or volunteer; do humanitarian work. Seeing the concerns of others will often put yours into perspective.

Occupy your mind with something that you feel passionate about. Have you noticed how quickly time passes when we are in love? Passion occupies us; we only think of him or her. So, discover what you feel passionate about and do it; you will have much less time to devote to worrying.

Do not make a mountain out of a molehill.

- Should you worry about how the housework is getting done less efficiently because you broke your heel?

- Will your son hate you when he grows up just because you forgot to pick up his birthday cake today?
- Will you get in trouble with your boss just because you just missed the subway and are late for work?

Get in the habit of taking less time to think.

Accept the fact that you sometimes think too much and for too long before acting. Once you catch yourself doing it, it will be much easier to curb the urge to overthink. It is possible, with time, to break this habit by giving yourself a deadline to stop thinking about something and take the appropriate action.

The longer you overthink, the more incredible opportunities that you will miss! Fear, especially the fear of failure, can prevent you from doing extraordinary things that can sometimes even change your life.

Failure can sometimes be valuable because it teaches us more about what we don't want. Through failure, we can learn more about ourselves and about the world around us. It's simple; the more you will fail in life, the more you will learn, and you will never make the same mistakes as in the past. You will be a person who has gained a lot of experience, and this experience will help you to succeed in the future.

Once we perceive ourselves as having less to lose by failing, some of the pressure that we tend to put on ourselves will lessen. Believe in yourself! You can accomplish many more things than you think.

Find an activity for occupying your mind.

Come on; it's time to get busy! Why? When you are occupied, you become so focused on the present moment and what you are doing that you are completely in control of your thoughts.

Take a walk or play sports! It will not only help you to reconnect with yourself, but it will help you stop overthinking. Exercise can provide a welcome distraction from what bills you have to pay or any other problems in your life.

You can also meditate to forget your worries. Living in the present moment is the best way to free yourself from your thoughts. You can also listen to a movie, read a book, dance, play outside, or go for a drink with a friend; these are other ways to occupy your mind.

I recommend doing one or more of the activities described above at least once a day. You won't regret it!

Get informed!

Feeling as if you have all the information that you need is essential to stop overthinking, and this information will make you more and more confident in your decisions! This confidence and information will also help to empower you to act more quickly.

For example, you can go and ask your friends for advice. Why? Well, since you have confidence in your friends or even your family, isn't this a great idea? What do you think? These people are here to help you; just ask them.

You can also do some research on Google to find answers to your questions. This will allow you to act much faster than before. Yes, even the Internet is an excellent way to find useful information to move forward.

Of course, you have to find the right information on

Google; it can be difficult to sort through the wealth of information on the internet. Make a habit of checking the sources of your information to make sure that you are on the right track.

BREATHE, BREATHE and RELAX

Whether you are at work, at home, or anywhere else, make it a habit to STOP at the first symptoms of stress and breathe slowly (and deeply) in and out.

Count from 5 to 1 while exhaling; focus on your breath. If that is not enough, repeat this exercise while counting from 10 to 1. Do this exercise as often as possible. If parasitic thoughts arise, let them pass and start counting again. You can also put your hands on your belly and feel your breath if this is easier for you.

Methods and Techniques to Stop Overthinking

The following ten tips are a compilation of the most helpful methods and techniques to stop overthinking. Some work better during the day and others work better for the evening.

It's best to pick three to five tips that best suit you and your situation and try them over the course of several days to weeks. If something does not work for you, try a different technique.

1. Write the thoughts out of your head.

Try journaling every night before going to bed. Write everything out of your head so that you do not have to hold onto it anymore.

If you come up with ideas more often when you fall asleep, put a notepad on the night table next to your bed, and write down the ideas immediately so that you can continue to sleep in peace afterwards.

2. Complete your to-do list the day before.

At the end of each day, write down your to-do list for the next day. This will help to keep you focused during stressful times and prevent thoughts and worries about work from disturbing you during the night.

3. Move your body.

Sports or exercise help to interrupt your thought carousel. When your thoughts overwhelm you during the day, put on music and dance around the room or do some sports.

If you have problems, especially when falling asleep, a walk before bedtime helps (strenuous exercise should be avoided because it keeps your body awake and not tired).

4. Have a soothing evening ritual.

An evening ritual will help you complete the day's work and help you to relax your mind before you go to sleep.

The ritual might look like this: Shut down your PC,

breathe deeply in and out three times, walk to your house and put on your favorites tunes. Alternatively, sports, meditation, swimming, and other active options are also suitable.

It is also essential that you start your evening at the same time each evening and do not work until the last minute before sleeping.

5. Become the observer of your thoughts.

The problem with pondering and thinking is that we are entirely absorbed by our thoughts. We become emotional, tense, anxious, angry, etc.

Unfortunately, switching off our thoughts does not work. But we can learn to become the passive observer of our thoughts. Then let the thoughts happen, but do not pursue them.

Just imagine that your thoughts are a play, which is performed on stage. In this scenario, you are a member of the audience, watching in interest as events unfold.

6. Think about what went well during your day.

When we remember the best and most positive events of our day, we allow the mind and body to relax. Just think about what went well during your day and was beautiful or enjoyable.

You can also imagine dream scenarios, such as a beautiful, enchanted garden or a peaceful island in the Pacific.

7. Use relaxation methods.

Basically, all forms of mindfulness, meditation and relaxation methods help. Much of it you can also teach yourself. You can learn online, for example, how to meditate correctly. Autogenic training, yoga or progressive muscle relaxation may also help you to fall asleep.

8. Use a thought-stopping method.

If the thoughts turn up again, stop and clap your hands loudly. You can also tell yourself, "Now is not the time.

I'll deal with you again tomorrow! Since many thoughts are very persistent, you'll probably have to repeat that a few times.

9. Listen to classical music.

Many classical songs have been proven to relax our brains and calm us down. Find a quiet, classic piece to fall asleep or incorporate classical music into your evening ritual in a different way.

10. Eliminate the root of the problem.

If you are currently being burdened with a particular issue that you keep thinking about, take the time to deal with it. Write it down. What could the solution look like? Who or what can support me? Where can I inform myself about possible solutions? What do I need to make this situation turn out better?

Eliminate causes of agitation. Behind the permanent tension we feel are often unprocessed fears, worries, crises and hardships. We cannot calm down because we are overburdened professionally or privately, have too much stress, or get emotionally stuck.

Therefore, we should not regard the problem as an enemy, but as a reliable indication that something needs to change in our lives. Then, it is essential to consider which problematic attitudes/behaviors/situations have led to our tension and how we can solve them permanently.

If you are too stressed, the solution may be to shorten or reduce commitments and make yourself a top priority in your life again. If you are too busy, ask others for help and seek their advice. Do you have too high demands on yourself and always try to perfect everything? Try to reduce your perfectionism. If you try to control things that are not within your control, you will always become frustrated. It is important to recognize your limits and learn to let go.

As you learn to focus on the underlying sources of your problems, you will be able to solve them more quickly.

Chapter 4

Positive/ Negative Thoughts and Effects

Stay positive, focus on what you can control, and stop worrying about tomorrow or the past.

Thinking is unavoidable! Nevertheless, that doesn't mean we can't control or limit ourselves to the type of thoughts that stream through our minds. Yes, every human — either old or young — is faced with the choice to think positively or negatively. Which method of thinking you choose should be based on your preference and what you would like to pursue as a goal.

Take, for instance, a person who wants to have a happier life. This person will be more likely to choose more positive, happier thoughts. But what is the best way to start doing this? Discipline, discipline, discipline! Once you start, you will notice how much happier you are when you choose positive thoughts.

Eventually, you will notice how capable you are of influencing your life solely by choosing more positive thoughts. When a person dwells more on negative thoughts; he/she is shifting their focus to what is negative. This can only have a negative impact on his/her life.

Letting negative thinking control your life will make you feel that you are worthless and that no one values or likes you; it will make you feel like giving up on life. But does that mean you will always be able to think positively all the time? No!

We are imperfect. None of us are immune to negative feelings. In our lives, there are dark times that bring sadness or fear, and when these times occur, maintaining positive thoughts may be difficult.

Nevertheless, no matter the level that life has driven you to, you have the sole responsibility to cultivate positive thoughts because they will assist you in overcoming that difficult situation. But you may wonder, why go on? What benefits will come from positive thoughts?

- They encourage you to seek solutions to your problems.
- They help you to learn from the past and proceed with life.

- They aid one's survival ability during tough times.
- They help people reach their goals and objectives.
- They boost happiness.
- They generate the high level of conviction that you need to surmount challenges.

Aren't these excellent benefits that project a person forward and have much potential to create joy in your life? Negative thoughts, on the other hand, can lead you to spend a lot of time worrying about possible negative life experiences instead of basking in the beauty of life.

Develop a positive outlook on life; that will help you to hit the ground running and prepare you to receive all of the good things that life has in store for you. Also, it will help to boost your personal development as you improve your physical, emotional, and financial well-being.

In order to help you to achieve positive thoughts, here are a few things to give in mind to help you attain a positive outlook on and receive more of the benefits that come from positive thinking.

Negative thoughts are often related to things like:

- Accusing others
- Complaining
- Worrying excessively
- Anger
- Feeling sorry for oneself

On the other hand, positive thoughts are related to things like:

- Studying
- Effective planning
- Problem-solving
- Goal setting
- Visualization
- Understanding

Frequently, self-help advice often includes messages of scrapping negative thoughts from our lives and increasing the positive thoughts that we have. That advice always sounds great; it looks like the best advice. Truthfully, negative thoughts are bound to wreck our lives, while it is believed that positive thoughts improve our lives overall.

Why does negative thinking occur? It usually involves using the brain excessively. And like the standard drain, overusing it might make it clogged. And when this happens, it becomes relatively easier to make bad decisions.

You Are Different From Your Thoughts

What do you most often think about? The chances are high that you will become that thing. In most cases, our thoughts often shape the pattern and direction of our lives.

What defines our life in most cases? It often depends on what we think about. But are we really our thoughts? Or are we different from our thoughts?

The fact that we can decide what we think about makes us different from our thoughts. We often think about certain conditions in our lives, and we feel like we can't just stop thinking about them. But that doesn't make us equal to our thoughts.

Unless you don't want to, we can change what we think about. We can switch that channel, but only if we are ready to do just that. If your thoughts always direct you, if you can't break off your thoughts, then you are on a journey with no definite destination. You only build more problems, you complicate issues, and you limit your progress.

Try to live in the present moment.

How to Live in the Present Moment

How should you go about living in the present moment? First, you have to see thinking as a tool. And like other tools, you don't need to use this tool whenever you are active. It should be used only when needed.

Overthinking can be stopped; you can break free from this negative pattern. But just how will you do that? Consider the following strategies:

- Always raise your awareness level.
- Your purpose will be defeated when you overthink. Let that be your motto.
- When your awareness level is raised, you should then start observing your thoughts.

- When you start thinking, your attention should be focused on how you are thinking and how this makes you feel. Most people don't want to feel unhappy, so if they are consciously choosing thoughts, these thoughts will be more likely to be positive. When they feel happy, they will be less likely to overthink things.

Your thinking sessions should be restricted to when they are most needed. What do I mean by this? At the start of the day, it is reasonable to set your daily priorities. Then you need to sit and think about what you have to accomplish that day. How long should that take? Maybe five to ten minutes. During this time, you can go through your thoughts and consider many options. But at the end of that time, ensure your mind is made up and that you have chosen a course of action. Achieving your goals should be your goal from that moment onward.

For every activity you are engaging in, you need to spend some time to think about them. But immediately after you are done thinking, take action, and then face your other essential tasks.

When will you enjoy your life?

If your mind is always filled with thoughts of your past or the future, when will you enjoy your life? Your past suffering and your future goals should not affect your present state. Appreciate each moment as long as you are alive.

Do you appreciate the fact that you are alive? If you do, then you will enjoy every moment and let go of thoughts that will make it hard for you to live in the moment. What do you love doing? Cooking? Dancing? Singing? Is it watching movies, visiting friends and family? Why not do it with your whole mind. Banish overthinking; it's a distraction that will take the fun out of each moment you spend engaging in your favorite activities.

Live each moment fully and enjoy it while it lasts. If you really want to enjoy your life, then you will need to start appreciating every moment.

Tips to Help You Attain a Positive Outlook on Life

Smile More Often

Have you ever heard that one of the best gifts to give a person is a smile? That's so true. Smiling doesn't cost you anything. Instead, it gives you a bright, welcoming outlook.

Researched conducted recently has confirmed that smiling has an incredible way of boosting one's mood. What lessons can be learned?

Smile often. If it doesn't come naturally to you, start first by forcing it. As you carry out your daily activities, think about a funny event or actions in the past, then generate a smile from there. Over time, you will master that art, and it will come naturally in your daily life. So in what instances should you smile? There is no specific rule, but these will help:

- At your workplace
- When someone walks past you
- While at home
- During a phone conversation

71

Something to Try: After reading this part, find a person to smile with!

Don't Dwell on Negative Thoughts

Negativity has a way of completely consuming you. It takes you away from the present moment. Sadly, many people spend excessive time — days, weeks, or even months — dwelling on negative thoughts. But what can you do in a situation where you find yourself in a fix?

Push away negative thoughts. Pause for a moment, and reflect on whether that thought helps you; you will surely realize that it doesn't. Then, ask yourself: Why would you dwell on something that is not beneficial? Then think of something worthwhile, something that might probably lift your mood.

Be Grateful for What You Have and Show It

You should not only be grateful for what you have, but you should show it.

It is easy to be happy when something pleasant occurs, but when bad times occur, it is often more difficult to focus on the things that you feel grateful for. During these times, you can become happier by focusing on the positive aspects of your situation or think of positive memories in your life to prevent negative thoughts. What can you be thankful for? It depends on your circumstances. But here are some things that you can be grateful for:

- Family
- Friends
- Your Job
- Good Memories
- Opportunities
- Being Alive

So, during a turbulent time, don't forget to think of things that you are grateful for. These things are often strong enough to repel negative thoughts and experiences.

Stay Bright in Each Bad Experience

It's been said that, in every bad situation, there are positive aspects. For example, someone has an accident: he/she loses his/her expensive smartphone or his/her money — probably the fund he or she owes to a debtor. Yes, that's an unfortunate incident, but is that all he/she can think of?

He can be grateful for the fact that he/she is alive and healthy! Additionally, positive thinking lets you turn negative experiences into life lessons, helping you identify your mistakes and preventing you from making the same ones twice.

In this way, you will be able to avoid some bad experiences since you will learn to do something differently next time, or you will be well prepared if a similar event occurs in the future.

Spend Quality Time with Positive-Minded Individuals

There are numerous thoughts and ideologies that many people carry about. Some are good, positive thoughts while some are with bad, negative ones. Those think negatively will likely attract mates with similar patterns of thinking, while positive-minded individuals will also attract people who think similarly. After all, birds of a feather flock together.

It could be helpful to cut off negative friends; that means spending less time with them and seeking out other, more positive individuals like yourself. Thus, you will be surrounded by positive thoughts.

If you spend more time with negative people, you feel bad, and are more likely to suffer from low self-esteem; on the flip side, spending time with more positive folks will help you to feel better about yourself!

Assist Others to Think Positively, Too

Positive thinking encourages you to be more supportive and encouraging to others; they will, in turn, become more positive as well. So how do you go about this?

Take just a few minutes and compliment someone, say hello today with a warm smile, perform loving gestures, and deliver pleasant cards to them. You never can tell to what extent these seemingly small acts of kindness will benefit them. Assuredly, when you put a smile on people's faces, you will be rewarded too.

Be More Optimistic

Optimism is a healthy trait, and, as such, should be cultivated by everyone. But it doesn't come naturally. One has to develop it first. So, even when you are faced with a negative situation, think of its positive aspects. Think of the good things that are around you and let them lift your mood and motivate you to take positive action.

What Negative Thoughts Do to Your Brain

When it comes to being happy, others can help, but the sole responsibility is yours! Sometimes you can't do away with a stressful situation, but how you let it define you is your choice. How do negative thoughts affect our thinking ability? Let me drive home this point with a brief example.

If you are walking down a lonely road and a lion jumps out suddenly, what comes to mind? Fear! That's natural; but after that fear, where should you go next? Run for safety, right? That's fine; what will most people dwell more on? Fear. But, to be realistic, what should be the primary goal? Safety, is that not so?

You see, this little highlighted illustration shows that negative thoughts do more harm; they impede critical thinking. Immediately, when the lion lands, you should think of fighting or climbing, but your fear may paralyze and prevent you from taking the necessary action to assure your own safety.

So, negative thoughts can block positive thoughts, hinder our goals, and prevent positive action. Foresight, which should be an added advantage to fighting any battle, becomes our worst enemy. On the other hand, let's quickly analyze the benefits that come from positive emotions or thoughts on the human brain.

The Effects of Some of Your Thoughts

For the purposes of this book, I conducted an experiment about overthinking and how it influences our emotional states. In the course of the experiment, the subjects were asked to divide into five different groups. Each group was shown a series of short video clips, which were designed to provoke a particular set of emotions.

The first group viewed pictures that caused an intense feeling of pleasure, while the second group viewed images that caused them to feel a sense of satisfaction.

The third group — the control group — served as the control experiment to compare the other variables. They were capable of seeing both positive and negative images that did not yield any results.

The last two groups were shown video clips depicting unpleasant emotions, while the fourth group was shown images that were designed to cause phobic reactions. In the fifth group, pictures were displayed that were designed to induce feelings of resentment.

In the long run, the participants were asked to self-reflect deeply when similar situations were presented to them and to write down whatever they decided to do about these situations. The participants in this exercise were given a book and a pen with about twenty empty spaces to jot things down. These phrases were to begin with the words, "I would like to…"

Upon observation, the groups that were shown images

designed to induce phobia and anger gave brief answers while, on the other hand, the group who had been displayed with pictures of pleasure, content and satisfaction wrote down many possible courses of action when compared to the categories used as the control group.

One can conclude, from this short experiment, that when you experience positive emotions — such as happiness, ecstasy and contentment — you're bound to see endless opportunities in your life to take action. This action, fueled by positivity, is much more likely to lead to good decisions and inspired action.

This is just the beginning; the benefits of positive thoughts do not subside after some brief moments of pleasure. As you continue reading, you'll be surprised at the extent to which the nature of our thoughts affect us.

Enhancing Your Skill Set Through Positive Thinking

A practical example using a real-life scenario

If your child loves playing outdoors, climbing trees, and spending time with their friends, there is every tendency that the child will develop skills that enable him or her to succeed in athletics and acquire swiftness, in addition to honing great communication skills while socializing with peers. On the other hand, he/she may love travelling and experiencing the world and possess certain skills that enable him to make new, creative discoveries. In both cases, the feelings of happiness and satisfaction that the child experiences as a result of these experiences will help him/her to be happier, leading him/her to think positive thoughts. People who have positive thoughts are always the happiest.

These positive thoughts will inspire your child to develop their skills further and acquire expertise in their chosen activity. After several years, you'll discover that the foundation of your child in athletics will be beneficial and may earn him or her an athletic scholarship. Your child's ability to communicate well may land him a job in a large company as a business manager. Their success will lead to even more positive thoughts. Their skills and abilities will pave the way for new discoveries as they inspire others and encourage them to think positively.

This is a phenomena is called being "wide and creative" and states that positive emotions broaden your thoughts, widen your chances, and help you to develop better skills, which are resources that improve the quality of an individual's life.

Negative emotions do just the opposite of this. Do you know why? Fear of the unknown and constant resentment makes all your efforts to develop skills and abilities for the future seem unrealistic and unattainable.

Many studies have asked the question: What is the secret to being positive always? As this book demonstrates, positive emotions play a significant role in bringing about and developing abilities, and that can bring us joy, possibly wealth, and inspire yet more positive thoughts.

How Can We Foster Positive Thoughts in Our Individual Lives?

How can we initiate the "wide and creative" concept in our everyday lives? By engaging in activities that prompt a feeling of joy, contentment and satisfaction will follow.

What works for you may be very different for someone else. It may be playing an instrument, spending quality time with people that make you laugh and amuse you, or engaging in hobbies that you love doing, such as catering or carving. You may also try one of these other three great ideas.

Meditation

Scientist Barbara Fredrickson discovered, together with her research mates, that people who ponder and contemplate things every day have more emotions than individuals who don't do this. Note also that individuals who are practical in their considerations tend to develop certain long-lasting abilities.

For instance, after about a period of three months from when they started conducting their research, it was noted that individuals who deliberate on a daily basis consistently show additional traits, such as increased determination, reduction in illnesses, increased consciousness of the things around them, and improved social skills.

Writing

Following the studies carried out, an experiment was conducted on 90 students divided into two categories. The first category discussed, in detail, over the course of three days, notable daily events, while the latter category discussed a restricted or controlled subject.

After a period of three months, the individuals in the first group who wrote about their thoughts and feelings about notable daily events showed mood elevation and a reduction in their rate of illness; they were seldom sick. However, writing down just three days of wonderful experiences can cause better health.

Play More Often

Make time to have fun and play more often. Often, we tend to plan conference meetings, business and other events in our itinerary without including time to play and hang out with friends or even visit a tourist attraction.

Take a few seconds now and think of the last time you dedicated as little as an hour to have fun and travel. When was the last time you created playtime? Make a schedule for yourself, dedicating ample time for just recreation, spending time with your friends, and other activities that serve no other practical purpose other than to bring you joy and contentment. This satisfaction will lead to positive thoughts and actions, which will help you to improve your abilities and your life.

Chapter 5

Ways to Attract Good Energy

Never expend your energy on worry; rather, use it to develop yourself and live a great life.

Positive energy can improve how we feel and communicate with the people around us. In our daily dealings with other people, we receive the kind of energy we send out. This energy is usually within our entire body, spirit and mind and, when it vibrates out, it's usually felt by others around us.

The way we feel about the people around us is a result of the kind of energy we carry around and the energy that we pick up on from them. We may feel free and cheerful being around some people and feel awkward and cold when we're around other people. Maintaining positive energy will improve our total well-being and help us to communicate more positively with people.

On the other hand, negative energy negatively affects our entire well-being due to the feelings of resentment, discord and unhappiness that accompany it. So, your ultimate goal should be to resist negative energy and embrace positive energy.

You can achieve this by increasing your energy level and surrounding yourself with positivity. Here are nine daily ways to help you boost your inner vibration and help you to feel the energy flow around you.

Pay Attention to the Energy You Release

If you're releasing lots of negative energy, there's no way you'll attract positive energy. How others feel when they are with you tells a lot about the kind of energy you discharge. Do people feel calm and happy or gloomy and sad when they're with you? Your answer to this will help you know if you have to work on boosting your energy or not.

Negative energy will always impact your relationships negatively, and your attitude towards others is a reflection of who you are. Ask yourself: What kind of impression do I make on people?

If you're the type that always reaches out to people and

creates great relationships, you may be releasing positive energy. If you're the type that people avoid, you may be releasing negative energy. Therefore, you must focus on emitting positive energy.

Change the Way You Think

If you spend most of your time thinking about negativity, you'll become a pessimist in no time. But if you spend most of your time thinking about the positive aspects of your life, no matter how hard that can sometimes be, you'll easily attract good things. Always ensure that the positive thoughts guide you in all you do.

If you're battling a bad situation, resist the urge to slip into pessimism. Instead, tell yourself that it's only a phase, and it will soon pass. Always engage in positive affirmations, especially when things go wrong. When you receive bad news, try not to dwell on it or catastrophize. Replace negative thoughts with positive ones. Let the inspiration for your actions come from positive and realistic thoughts about yourself.

Discard Negative Influences

Quit surrounding yourself with negative people, things or places will take away your happiness and total well-being. Some people are toxic, and you should be far away from them. These are people that always try to discourage you from everything that you do and look for every means to constantly bring you down. If you're not observant enough, you may begin to pick up bad habits from these toxic places, people or things.

When you disengage yourself from these negative influences, you'll be able to design the kind of life you want for yourself. At times, disentangling from these influences may seem difficult because they're a part of your daily life. If this is the case, avoid them at all costs and prepare yourself mentally if you cannot avoid running into them.

Increase Your Circle

As you discard negative influences, increase your circle of positive influences. Surround yourself with people of like minds that can influence you positively and inspire you to be the best you can be. Ensure that you hold these relationships in high esteem and nurture them.

These people should be able to be honest and authentic with you, but it shouldn't be done to spite you or make you feel less sure of yourself. The positive energy that radiates from this group will help you live a happier life.

Be Kind and Compassionate

Some little acts of kindness can have a significant impact on the receiver and the giver. Being kind and compassionate towards others has been proven to attract lots of positivity and good relationships. So, the more you give and show compassion to others, the better your physical and mental well-being will be.

Being kind is also a great way to motivate the people around you and inspire them to be kind to others. Smiling to people around you, serving someone a cup of tea or doing anything that makes people around you happy sends loads of positive energy to you, and this boosts your inner happiness.

Be Grateful

Each day, if you dwell too much on negative thoughts, you'll find it hard to see the things you ought to be grateful for. Devote most of your quiet time to thinking about the little things in your life and be thankful for them. Doing this will help you let go of harmful and toxic emotions.

Think of the good things and people in your life and why you are grateful for them. Doing this for a few minutes every day will help you a great deal. If you can't think of any right now, you can begin by keeping a gratitude journal and jotting down a list of things that make you happy and feel contented. Being grateful will help you reflect on the bad times you've had and how you overcame them all.

Discover Your Inner Strength

Taking your focus away from all the negative thinking that may erode your confidence level and cause feelings of insecurity and self-doubt and shifting to positive thinking that boosts your self-esteem and confidence is essential to developing inner strength. Inner strength is what will make you resilient in the face of stressful situations and help boost your energy level so that you can handle whatever comes your way.

Align Your Current Self With Your Future Self

The things you spend your time and money on will determine how far you'll go in life. These choices you make today will shape your life tomorrow. Ask yourself: What do I desire most in the world? Work towards being the person that your future self will be proud of by building healthy relationships and a healthy lifestyle.

Develop a picture in your mind of who you would like to be in the future and start taking steps to make it a reality. Doing this will help you exert more control over your life, and the more positive actions you take, the more positive the reality you will create for your future self.

Act in Good Faith

There's a general belief in business that both parties act in good faith as they work together. We all benefit from treating one another fairly, but only a few people understand that this principle should be followed as we interact daily personally or professionally.

Endeavour to be nice to everyone you meet and treat them with respect, and in most cases, you'll receive the same gesture. Even if someone wrongs to you, avoid retaliation as it won't make you feel better. They may be having a bad day and react negatively to you for this reason. So, when you act nicely to everyone, even when they react harshly to you, you can be sure to attract positive energy, and this will help a lot.

Chapter 6

Coping with Worrying

Worry is the interest you pay in advance for the loan you may never take out.

Do you always have to deal constantly with worries and anxiety? Here are some useful tips to help ease your anxiety and calm your troubled mind.

How much is too much?

It is very normal to experience worries, anxiety and doubts in daily life. It is our reaction to it which makes the greatest difference in our lives. It's very natural to get worked up about a first date, an upcoming interview, or an unpaid bill. Becoming frequently worried becomes overwhelming when it is uncontrollable and persistent. If every day you become worked up by picture all of the negative things that might happen to you, you are letting anxious thoughts interfere with your life and well-being.

Negative thoughts, incessant worrying, and constantly

expecting poor outcomes will have a negative effect on your physical and emotional well-being. It gradually weakens you emotionally, taking your strength and leaving you restless and nervous, with headaches, insomnia, muscle tension and stomach problems.

The effect of this on your personal life, your concentration at school and work cannot be overemphasized. For some people, it's easier to take out their frustration on your loved ones and people closest to them, take alcohol or drugs or try to distract themselves by tuning out from everything.

Chronic anxiety and worry is a sign of Generalized Anxiety Disorder (GAD), a disorder that causes restlessness, nervousness and tension, together with a feeling of unease which can take over your life.

If you feel burdened by tension and worries, you can take a few steps to take your mind off anxious thoughts. Over time, worrying constantly becomes a problem. It becomes a mental habit when prolonged and is very difficult to break. Train your brain to be calm and think only positive thoughts, and change your outlook on life to a more relaxed and confident perspective.

Why is it so hard to quit worrying?

Worrying constantly does nothing but affect your life negatively. It keeps you up at bedtime and makes you edgy and tense in the daytime. You may detest the feeling of being nervous and confused, but it's very difficult to stop worrying. Beliefs about worrying, either positive or negative, fuel this nervousness further and may cause additional anxious thoughts in chronic worriers.

Negative Beliefs About Worrying

Most people believe that getting worried constantly is very harmful to your health and can drive you nuts. You may be worried about losing control over your thoughts and worries, fearing that they'll consume you and never stop. Negative beliefs about worrying may further fuel your anxiety, but positive beliefs about worrying can do as much harm.

Positive Beliefs About Worrying

You may believe, either consciously or unconsciously,

that you can prevent bad things from happening to you, prepare for the worst and foster solutions. Probably, you keep convincing yourself that by worrying about a particular thing for a long time, you'll be able to figure it out eventually.

If you're convinced that getting worried is the most responsible thing to do in such a situation and the only way to avoid overlooking anything, it's even more difficult to break the habit. When you come to the realization that worrying is not the solution but the problem itself, you will be capable of gaining control of your mind.

How to Quit Worrying

Tip 1: Choose a Short Period Each Day to Worry

It can be quite difficult to be productive when your thoughts are consumed by worry and anxiety, distracting your attention from school, work, or your family. In this case, the strategy of putting off worrying can actually do a lot of good. Instead of getting rid of these thoughts, grant yourself permission to have these thoughts later on in your day.

Dedicate a period for worry each day. Set up a time and place to think of things that bother you. It should be at the same time every day (for example, 6 p.m. to 6:15 p.m. in the bedroom). Choosing a timeframe that won't affect your bedtime and or create additional anxiety in your life. During this period, you can worry about whatever you want. The rest of the day should be classified as worry-free.

Put down your worries in writing. When you find yourself thinking anxious or worrying thoughts, simply note them briefly and continue with your daily activities. Always remind yourself that there's time for you to think about it later; there is no need to get worked up about them now.

Take a look at your worry list during your scheduled worry period. If your thoughts still bother you, let yourself think about those things, but only for your specified worry period. You'll notice that, as you examine your worries in this manner, it's easier to establish a more balanced outlook to worrying. If, at this point, your worries don't seem as important as they used to, simply reduce the length of your worry period and enjoy your day to the fullest.

Tip 2: Challenge Anxious Thoughts

The way that you look at the world may be altered a bit if you are a chronic worrier and thinker. It changes everything, and you may tend to feel threatened. For instance, you picture only a worst-case scenario, and you assume the worst or handle your anxious thoughts as if they were facts.

As a result, you may not feel secure enough to tackle daily challenges head- on; you may assume that you'll lose it at the slightest sign of trouble. Such thoughts, also known as cognitive distortions, include: "All-or-nothing" thinking, having a black-and-white perspective, concluding that "If it isn't perfect, then I'm a complete failure", or "I wasn't hired for this job; I'll never get any job again". You may make a generalization from just one negative experience and expect it to be true forever. Life doesn't work that way.

You may notice only the things that went wrong in your day, instead of things that went well, resulting in thoughts such as: "I didn't get the last test question; I'm stupid, and I can't do anything right.". You may attribute positive events to sheer luck, rather than your own ability to create positive outcomes.

You may take your assumptions for facts. You may make yourself a mind- reader or fortune teller with thoughts like: "I just know something bad will happen" or "I know she secretly hates me". This creates bad energy. Without faith, your mind may automatically jump to worst-case scenarios, such as: "The plane is experiencing turbulence; it's going to crash". You may take your thoughts for reality: "I feel so stupid; I'm the laughingstock now."

You may make a list of your dos and don'ts and beat yourself up when you default on any of the rules, with thoughts such as, "I shouldn't have gone there. Now I look like such a fool". You may label yourself based on your shortcomings and mistakes, with thoughts such as, "I can't do anything right; I should be a loner". You may take responsibility for things that are beyond your control, thinking: "It's my fault my son died. I shouldn't have left him alone by the pool."

Challenging These Thoughts

Try this out. Challenge these negative thoughts during your worry period, and ask yourself these questions:

- What evidence proves that these thoughts are valid or not?

- Is there a better way to look at this situation? A better and more positive way?

- What are the chances of my fears becoming a reality? What are the probabilities? What are some likely outcomes in this situation?

- Are these thoughts helpful? How do they affect me? Do they help me or hurt me?

- What's my advice to a friend who has been in a similar situation?

Tip 3: Differentiate the Solvable Worries From the Unsolvable Worries

Studies have shown that you experience less anxiety when you worry. While you think about the problem in your head, you're distracted from your emotions for a while and feel like you're actually solving a problem; in reality, getting worried and problem-solving are two different things altogether.

By problem-solving, you are examining a situation, thinking of solid ways to deal with it, and putting these plans into action. On the other hand, worrying seldom leads to any solutions. The more time that you spend thinking of worst-case scenarios, the less prepared that you are to handle them if they actually happen. That's the simple truth.

Is your worry solvable?

There are different types of worries; some have solutions, while others don't. Solvable worries are those that you can act to resolve instantly. For instance, when you're preoccupied with your debts, you can call a friend or relative to settle your debts, with the option to repay them later.

This type of worry can also be described as productive worry. On the other hand, those worries that do not have a corresponding action can be characterized as unsolvable problems; for instance, thoughts like: What if I get leukemia someday? What if my family gets involved in an accident?

In a situation where you can take action about the thing getting you worried, begin to look for solutions. Compile a list of all the ways you feel that you can solve your worry. Don't get caught in searching for the one perfect answer to the problem.

Concentrate on those things within your reach that can

be changed instead of brooding over situations that are out of reach. After deciding upon the solution that will solve your problem, develop an action plan. Immediately you set out to address your fear; you will be less worried.

On the other hand, when the worry is not something you can solve, make peace with yourself by being at ease with the uncertainty. For people who worry excessively, many of their fears tend to be along these lines. People tend to worry when they are trying to anticipate the future, and this is done to feel more in control and prevent potential problems.

However, the bitter truth is that worrying doesn't solve anything; life is occasionally unpredictable. So why not enjoy your life now instead of being engrossed in unpleasant things that have not taken place?

Most people long for inner peace: the feeling that everything is, and will be, all right. But sometimes, we worry, develop fears, and ponder the same things over and over without finding a way out.

The tragic thing is that, of course, we know rationally that the upcoming test is not a life-and-death situation. Our child is probably not lying in the ditch just because he/she does not call at the agreed-upon time. Our dull headache is probably harmless and not the symptom of a brain tumor.

But when our anxiety rises, we think in circles or worry about failing, and we lose that realistic perspective. We are like under a "black cloud". Then we can only imagine all that has happened or is going to happen. We only see what is going wrong in our lives, family, company, and in the world. These thoughts are, in fact, only thoughts — but we lose our perspective.

Do you imagine disastrous, unpredictable things might occur? What is the possibility that these things will actually happen? Even when the probability that bad things will happen is low, do you still worry over the little chance that something terrible will occur?

Tune into your emotions and thoughts and observe them. You can overcome your worries by observing your feelings and thoughts while staying rooted in the present moment. Find out from your loved ones how they combat their uncertainty about things. Can you follow their strategies to overcome your worries?

Tip 4: Interrupt the Worry Cycle

Answer the following questions:

- What am I worried about?
- What possible solutions exist?
- Which solution should I choose?
- How and when do I implement the solution?

Just writing down your worries can provide you with some relief. If you then also write down different solutions, you will see your fears in a different light. You will adopt the observer perspective and will be able to think more logically about what you can do.

Meditate. Meditation helps to alleviate daily worries by shifting our attention. We focus only on the here and now and can leave the concerns of the past or future behind. Similarly, meditation can also help us observe ourselves and understand our negative thought patterns. We only need to find a comfortable, quiet place and focus carefully on our breathing. Various studies have shown that meditating not only helps to ease worries but can also reduce stress and anxiety.

Practice progressive muscle relaxation. Sports and exercise also promote relaxation and sleep. They also help to distract us from our everyday worries and promote our self-esteem and well-being. This confidence will make it easier for us to address our worries head-on. Also, researchers claim that exercise can reduce not only anxiety but also improve our emotional well-being and energy. Many scientists believe that physical activity can significantly reduce depression.

Tip 5: Talk about your worries.

One way to worry less is to talk to our closest friends about what is bothering us. When we are worried, friends can help us to alleviate our fears and see things from a different perspective. They can help us to look at the problem from the outside. Then, we can often find a solution or come to realize that it's not as bad a problem as we feared. When they listen without judgment or criticism and pay attention to what we say, their empathy can help us to feel calmer and more relaxed.

Having someone listen to us with empathy is essential to make us feel better. Even professional help is very beneficial, in some cases, if you cannot find a way out yourself.

Tip 6: Practice Mindfulness

Most people think of mindfulness as sitting quietly with their eyes closed, breathing deeply in a meditative state. However, meditation is just one example of mindfulness. Mindfulness is an exercise that does not isolate you from your current environment but makes you more aware of the situation where you find yourself; it is the practice of unbiased awareness.

Mindfulness is the experience of being in the present. You accept things as they are, without judging whether they are positive or negative or how they should be. If you are mindful, with all of your five senses, you are open to the world as it is, without distraction and reflection on the past or fears about the future. Being mindful means experiencing the present with a beginner's spirit, as if you were experiencing it for the first time.

Acknowledge and observe your worries. Instead of trying to get over your fears, watch your thoughts like a stranger without passing judgment. Stay focused on the present moment. Avoid getting lost in your thoughts and concentrate on the feelings and thoughts that cross through your mind. And, in the event that you get lost in your thoughts, bring your attention back to your current environment.

Repeat daily. Ensure you continuously practice mindfulness to be at ease with yourself.

How to Practice Basic Mindfulness Meditation

Create a suitable place.

It is ideal if you have a designated area for mediation. After some time, your mind switches to relaxation mode whenever you enter that area. A suitable meditation place should be nicely furnished. If you do not want to set up a permanent location, it is sufficient to use a specific mat or pillow every time you meditate. Meditating in a particular spot will often do you a lot of good.

Wear comfortable clothes.

Nothing is more annoying than a pinching waistband or too-tight collar during meditation. Such small disturbing factors detract from the calming power of meditation and are really unpleasant. Therefore, make sure you wear comfortable clothing that does not restrict you. It should also match the temperature so that you will not feel cold even if you stay motionless for a while.

Eliminate distractions.

During your exercise, you should not be disturbed. Therefore, tell your family members that you would prefer to be left alone for the moment or choose a time when you are alone in the house. Turn off your cell phone or put it in another room where you cannot hear it. Ideally, you also turn off the doorbell. Then you can start your meditation exercise undisturbed.

Choose a meditation posture.

The typical meditation posture is a variation of the cross-legged position. It does not have to be that way; you can, for example, sit on a chair or kneel on the floor with a meditation cushion.

Even when lying down, meditation is quite possible, but there is a risk that you may fall asleep quickly, which is, of course, not the point of meditation. When sitting or kneeling, make sure that your back is as straight and upright as possible.

Start with short meditation sessions.

Hours of meditation are hardly feasible at the beginning and usually very unpleasant for inexperienced meditators. Such a long duration is unnecessary. Units of five or ten minutes are enough to start with.

Turn off your thoughts.

Almost all meditations are about calming your thoughts. What sounds so simple can be very difficult. In the beginning, you will probably catch yourself becoming distracted by your thoughts. This is completely normal. You mustn't get angry; you will just become more distracted. Put the thought away lovingly, and return to your exercise. Gradually, it will become easier for you.

Practice regularly.

As with many other things, meditation requires regular exercise. The more you meditate, the easier it will be for you, and the more deeply relaxed that you will become. It would be ideal to practice daily; however, two to three training sessions per week is also great.

Chapter 7

Strategies to Reduce Stress and Curb Anxiety

No amount of anxiety can alter the future! Leave no room for anxiety in your mind.

You can practice a relaxation method like progressive muscle relaxation because people who display generalized anxiety often have high levels of responsiveness.

Take up short-term activities that are captivating and enjoyable to take your mind off certain things and distract it from certain negative thoughts. These could be activities that have been useful in the past. Exercise is a vital tool for managing worry. When you exercise, brain chemicals are released that counteract low moods, worry and anxiety. Exercise also acts as a distraction from worries and reduces nervousness. Exercise at least once a day for half an hour, with cardio exercises at least three days a week.

Incorporate organized problem-solving strategies to

handle stressors that contribute to your worry. When challenged with a difficult situation or life problem, most people often don't know how to handle these difficulties and lack enough coping skills; they feel as if they're incapable of controlling what they're faced with. Such feelings cause people to worry.

Everyone has problems and challenges in their lives, but they are more visible and difficult to handle if you always get worried. A useful strategy to combat this is training in organized problem-solving. Efficient problem- solving techniques minimize, reduce, control and even prevent worrying in our daily lives.

Avoid activities and situations that foster anxiety by confronting your fears and facing them directly but gradually. For instance, you could place them in a hierarchy, depending on which step you fear the most. These fears could be:

1. Arriving late for a meeting
2. Not checking your mobile phone for one hour
3. Going grocery shopping without a shopping list
4. Planning a birthday party
5. Accepting an invitation without checking with your calendar
6. Going out without your mobile phone for the

day

Adopt Cognitive Interventions

There are two errors that those who have GAD tend to make:

Overestimation: They are always on edge, overestimating the likelihood of catastrophe. For example, they think thoughts like: "This will be a disaster!" or "I had better prepare for the worst scenario".

Underestimation: They are often underestimating their ability to cope with their problems. For instance, they might think thoughts like, "I will have a breakdown." or "I won't be capable of dealing with this situation".

If you have a problem with thoughts like these, what can you do? Simple! Challenge these negative thoughts by mastering how to recognize thoughts that are distressing and whether these thoughts are realistic.

For example, you may have to ask yourself what

evidence you have to support these thoughts. If you can't find any, you may not need to dwell on it. Also, it might be that the best thing to do is to identify how likely it is that your fears for the future will come true.

Furthermore, folks with GAD should also continually work at challenging their beliefs and assumptions regarding themselves. For instance, a person's worry could be that he will never get prepared on time, and this might be followed up with the assumption that if things go wrong, he should be blamed and the creeping belief that he or she is a failure. Even though some believe that worry prevents harmful occurrences, this is inaccurate. Instead, it increases one's level of anxiety.

Well, as soon a person has been able to identify and question his or her negative thoughts, then the next line of action is shifting attention away from the negative thoughts. Cognitive Behavioral Therapy assists in identifying and challenging these assumptions and helping individuals to develop alternative beliefs that are healthier and better for their personal well-being. Experiences have shown that mindfulness-based interventions will also aid you to remain focused.

Adopt Emotion Regulation and Mindfulness

Recent studies have suggested that worry may present itself as a way of doing away with emotional processing. Involve yourself in what is called emotion-regulation strategies and mindfulness skills, as these will boost the form and manner in which you identify and experience underlying emotions.

Do away with the use of medications that will sedate you. Don't binge to relieve your anxiety. They may provide temporary relief from anxiety, but frankly, it will come back later. Instead of doing these, set up a time to consult a specialist or go for CBT if symptoms occur for longer than three months regardless of the above measures.

Realistic Ways to Cope With Symptoms of Anxiety and Excessive Worrying

It's great to learn tips and tricks that we can use to wrestle anxiety and excessive worry. Each time that you find yourself in an unpleasant situation, ask yourself these simple but effective questions.

- Is my worry reasonable?
- Will what I fear actually happen?
- How can I be sure that what I fear will happen?
- Could there be any other plausible explanation or outcome in my situation?
- Am I trying to predict things in the distant future that I am unable to do something about?
- If this worst-case scenario occurs, will it really be as bad as I think that it will be?
- Is it worth worrying about?
- How would someone else view my worry?

What is the Effect of Thinking the Way That You Do?

What will be the effect of thinking the way that you are thinking right now? Do these thoughts make you feel empowered to solve the problem at hand or do they discourage you from believing in yourself and feeling capable of facing the problem at hand? Are there instances where your worries are valid? Yes! Sometimes we worry about things that are likely to happen. In this situation, what you will need to do is to face your worry and do something about it if you can.

If not, you may need to let it go. For those who are experts when it comes to worrying, this may seem impossible. However, you could say to yourself, "There is absolutely nothing that could be done to alter this right now". Then you can find some other activity to occupy your mind and distract you from this situation that you have no control over.

Is There a True Problem to Solve?

If there really is a problem to solve, then you might

have to focus your attention on a practical solution for it. In this case, you might turn to problem-solving skills to deal head-on with the things that are worrying you.

Below are six structured problem-solving techniques that you can use to do this:

1. Write down precisely what you think the real problem is.
2. Write down all the possible solutions that you could think of; don't eliminate the bad ones yet.
3. Consider each solution carefully and logically.
4. Select the most practical solution.
5. Plan carefully how you will work on that solution.
6. Do it.

Note: Anxiety is not your fault. Daily life and comes with stressors that can affect a person's thoughts, feelings, and everyday functioning!

10 Things That You Might Not Realize Can Be Signs of Anxiety

It is normal to worry. Everyone is worried at one time or another, most often with discernment. After all, being aware of possible dangers leads us to take logical actions, such as paying attention before crossing a street! But it is certainly possible to worry too much.

If, one day, someone discovers a lump in his/her throat, one will most certainly be worried. We will feel panic, discomfort, and anxiety; we may decide to react, to search the internet for information, to make an appointment with a doctor, and to subject ourselves to a multitude of exams to know what it is. Our thoughts race: What if it's cancer? What if there is no treatment? Will we die? As we catastrophize, we are already experiencing disaster, with all the physical and psychological impressions of anxiety associated with it, which leaves us feeling tired and demoralized.

In the first situation, our anxiety remains productive. Founded on something concrete — there is a ball that could affect our lives — it helps us make decisions, solve hardships, and deal with danger. In the second case, anxiety paralyzes us. Often, we worry without effectively setting up guidelines to solve the problem.

Are you convinced that worrying is an ingrained feature of your personality? That worrying about your financial situation, your health, the health of others, your work, your family, your friends, your safety, crime, etc. is altruism? That by considering the worst, you preserve yourself?

Here are some signs that indicate that you are anxious:

You're always busy, but you can never seem to get things done.

If you are unable to complete a job or perform a task as planned, you panic, and you constantly seek reassurance and reassurance.

Catastrophic existential thoughts plague you.

You always expect the worst. For example, your spouse is late. He was at a meeting that may have been run late, but the worst scenarios haunt you. You are convinced that he has been in some sort of accident, has contracted a possible illness, or some other calamity has occurred.

You're easily startled.

In a situation where you are startled easily, there is a need to become more aware of your emotions. Research has established that if you are anxious, you have an increased level of being startled by everyday occurrences, such as a door slamming or a car backing up.

Your stomach is upset, but your doctor can't figure out why.

If constantly begin to have stomach problems, an have eliminated food poisoning and other stomach illnesses, your stomach upset could be the result of anxiety. You can become sick to your stomach due to anxiety.

You're a perfectionist.

Although being a perfectionist is not a worrisome thing, the inability to go outside your comfort zone to avoid mistakes can be a sign of anxiety. If, when you venture outside your comfort zone, you don't achieve what you want, and you begin to feel ashamed and inferior, this is a sign of anxiety due to perfectionism.

It has been pointed out by experts that perfectionists tend to reject help, even when they are worried that they may fail.

Everyone around you is getting on your nerves.

It is important to relax after a long day. Anxiety often prevents you from doing so. At this point, you may become easily irritated at any action from your friends or relatives. If you feel like this, the possibility that you are feeling anxious is very high.

When you feel uneasy or anxious, look for a physical activity that you like to do or something else to distract your mind.

You are incapable of making decisions.

Another sign of anxiety is the emotional attachment becoming too overwhelmed to make decisions. You get bogged down when considering the possible consequences of your decision, and you get stuck in between several different choices.

You cannot sleep.

Anxiety often disturbs our sleep, which is one of the most important things necessary to stay healthy. Without a night of good sleep, we put our health and our life in danger. For example, driving while we are sleep-deprived becomes as dangerous as when we drive after drinking alcohol.

You may become very restless in many cases and suffer because of increasing sleep disorders.

You're having random chills or hot flashes.

In a situation where you begin to suffer from chills and hot flashes without being sick, it can be as a result of anxiety. You should consult your doctor to understand the concept of generalized anxiety disorder.

Also, when you have nightmares and flashbacks, which remind those affected of the traumatic experiences and trigger traumatic memories that would otherwise have long been forgotten, these are also signs of anxiety.

You feel like you have failed at life.

Perhaps the worst feeling that can show that you are worried is when you begin to feel like you are not good enough for the world. You begin to feel useless to your loved ones and even at work. If you are constantly feeling this way, then you are likely to have an anxiety disorder.

Chapter 8

Embracing Mindfulness as an Efficient Alternative to Overthinking

Worrying blurs your mind and prevents you from seeing clearly. Instead, embrace mindfulness.

What's Mindfulness?

In simple terms, mindfulness is the average ability of a man to be completely conscious of his current location and what he is doing in that location and not being distracted by what goes on within his environment.

Naturally, everyone is blessed with the concept of mindfulness within them; notwithstanding, it can only be accessed when it's consistently used. But how do you know you've become mindful? You become conscious of what is going through your brain. When you consistently teach your mind to be mindful, you redesign your brain.

Further, the aim of mindfulness is to be conscious of their inner operations of the function of the brain, its physical processes and feelings. If, by chance or knowingly, we lose grip on the critical things in life, life may leave us behind. With mindfulness, we can be more present, more aware, and more capable of dealing with life.

How People Define Mindfulness

Some have defined mindfulness as a condition of being conscious of one's current situation. They say that individuals who do not judge situations as either good or bad are not being controlled by their thoughts and that these individuals can be tagged as being mindful.

Being mindful is a useful tool to help one understand and control subconscious feelings that may present big problems in both our work and personal relationships. Mindfulness suggests being in the current moment instead of dwelling on the past or peering into an unknown existence. As a tool, mindfulness has been defined by many to be utilized during meditation.

Many see mindfulness as therapeutic. There are a series of advantages to being mindful. Some of these benefits include reducing a person's level of anxiety and depression and boosting a person's general well-being, helping them to combat feelings of isolation and rejection.

The Best Way to Lead a Mindful Life

A person's emotional condition determines their ability to remain objective in stressful situations. Dwelling on painful memories and past events can haunt people and prevent them from doing their very best within their individual environments.

A man or woman may have, many years ago, done something wrong, and years after year, the thought will keep returning and haunting him or her. He may want something to happen that will take away the thought of remembering that occasion. But how could that be solved?

This person would need to focus on that reality that is existing within his/her environment, and not let his past regrets disturb his/her present happiness. There is no doubt that the best tool to help a person to be conscious of what happens within his or her environment is mindfulness; it enables us to stop judging whether the situation is good or bad.

If you really want to control your feelings, mindfulness is something you should practice.

Important Facts to Know About Mindfulness

These mindfulness facts are important for you to know. Knowing them will allow you to understand mindfulness and appreciate its functions.

Fact 1: Mindfulness is not a myth or farce.

Developing mindfulness is a scientifically-proven method which will result in improved relationships with friends, neighbors, families, coworkers, and other individuals.

Fact 2: You need not alter your personality.

We don't need to change anything about our personality to become capable of being present. Changing who you are will achieve little or no success at all; methods like these are bound to fail. But with mindfulness, you can bring the best out of yourself and become a new, improved you.

Fact 3: Everyone can learn mindfulness.

Mindfulness is gained by learning and practicing. And it is very easy; anyone can learn how to become more mindful.

Fact 4: Mindfulness is a way of life

Mindfulness is not just common practice; it is a way of life. This way of life helps us to get rid of mindless stress and handle life's challenges more easily.

Fact 5: Evidence supports the benefits of mindfulness.

The effects and benefits of mindfulness have been observed in scientific studies and in the personal experiences of those who practice it. These studies indicate that mindfulness improves health, general well-being, and all other aspects of human lives.

Fact 6: Mindfulness gives birth to innovation.

Mindfulness eliminates mental clutter and frees the mind up for creative and intellectual pursuits. You will find it easier to provide answers to complex situations and problems.

Fact 7: There Are Some Mindfulness Practice Basics

With mindfulness, your reaction to daily events becomes more positive. Self-control is improved, making the impact of mindfulness more beautiful.

Wondering how to go about practicing mindfulness? Here are some important steps to follow;

- Set aside time and space for your practice.

For effective mindfulness practice, it is best to schedule a regular time and place. Always set time and space aside for this task.

- Do not pass judgement on your thoughts.

The chances that we will judge our thoughts while

practicing mindfulness are high. The right thing to do is to observe such thoughts without passing judgement.

- Have a positive view of the present moment.

The goal of mindfulness is not only to achieve unmatched calmness and quietness; it is actually to increase our attentiveness to each moment, without judging it to be good or bad. Hard as it may be, the goals of mindfulness are achievable.

- Accept each moment as it is.

We might easily get lost in thought. The best way to come back to the present is through mindfulness.

- Stop your mind from wandering mindlessly.

At every moment, numerous thoughts will pop into your head. But never let these thoughts be the basis for your judgment. Identify the point at which your mind starts to wander and refocus it on the present moment.

These following practices will help you achieve mindfulness more easily. They are simple, but you must be dedicated and work hard to bring about positive results.

Mindful Practices to Help You Improve Your Life

A positive change in attitude and the effectiveness of your activities increase when you can set time aside each week to practice mindfulness or mindful exercise. This exercise will help you to become more patient and better tolerate others. Your mind will worry less about criticism or negative comments. It will result in you socializing more easily and becoming friendly.

The result will definitely affect your sleep. You will get a sound and peaceful night's rest. Overall, your day will be eventful, happy, and you will feel fulfilled long into the evening.

Mindful Walking

Think about what you want to do for 15 to 20 minutes each day while walking. This is mindful walking. Since walking helps to keep you refreshed and improve thinking, mindful walking has a definite purpose. To get better results, it is best to stick to a particular pattern and method. This will enhance your progress.

You need to be attentive and concentrate well if you are engaging in mindful practices. Endeavor to pay attention to even the littlest of details, such as the people and events around you. Four essential elements will make mindful walking possible: a steady pace, relaxed gaze, straight posture, and good balance.

Posture

The success of mindful walking is influenced by your posture. You need to hit that perfect position while you engage in mindful walking. Getting the right posture involves releasing your body into each moment. Getting rid of stiffness, standing in an upright position, and ensuring that your feet are planted firmly on the ground. This will help you to walk better.

Balance

To avoid distraction while engaging in mindful walking, you need to have the right balance. This balance should be obvious from your finger down to your arms, and even to your tummy.

You may need to do this in order to be successful; bend

the left thumb and wrap the other finger around it. Then place it on your stomach. Now place the right hand on it, and let your right thumb rest in-between the left thumb and the index finger.

Gaze

Your gaze level affects your attentiveness to things around you, and how well you concentrate. More success is achieved when you lower your gaze; don't necessarily look at the ground, though. Remove or lower your gaze when you start to become too focused on the things that you see around you.

Pace

During mindful walking, your pace is another thing to consider. Walking too fast will help you achieve nothing. Try a steady pace; walk slowly, or at least below your average walking pace. When your feet touch the ground, it will help you to feel more grounded in the moment and able to concentrate.

Why Should You Practice Mindfulness?

There are many misconceptions about mindfulness. Therefore, people who start engaging in mindfulness often find that the results are very different from what they expect or from what they have been promised.

Below are some of six most frequent misconceptions about mindfulness:

- The goal of mindfulness is to make you a better person.
- The goal of mindfulness is to halt your ideas.
- Mindfulness is a religious practice.
- Mindfulness will protect you from being affected by real-life conditions.
- Mindfulness will solve all your problems.
- The goal of mindfulness does not go beyond eliminating stress.

Yes! Mindfulness helps people to deal with their stress, but that is not the main objective of mindfulness. What then, is the goal? It is to ensure that you are conscious about what is happening around you: things happening in the physical, mental and emotional faculties. Start

137

learning mindfulness today for the following reasons:

Train Your Body to Thrive Via Mindfulness

One thing that has helped athletes to surpass their own expectations, achieve greatness, and rid themselves of negativity is mindfulness. Their training often involves channeling their strength in the best possible way and gaining better control of their breathing.

Athletes can attain full presence and achieve their goals when they work on a mix of mindfulness, which includes tactical breathing, and intellectual behavioral exercises.

Boosting Your Creativity via Mindfulness

By becoming more mindful, you can clear your mind, freeing yourself up to become more creative in all of your daily tasks or assignments.

Strengthen Your Neural Connection via Mindfulness

The development of new neural routes and building new connections in the brain can be made possible through the practice of mindfulness. This improves your abilities and helps you concentrate more on things that are currently happening around you. It also helps you become more flexible and promotes well-being.

Chapter 9

Minimalism for Anxiety Relief

Never allow little things to occupy your mind; live a simple life.

Exploring Decluttering for Relieving Anxiety

Minimalism: What does it mean?

Minimalism refers to a conscious situation or condition of having lesser belongings. A minimalist sees minimalism as a conscious condition, which is often driven by purpose, intentionality, and clarity.

Minimalism helps us to reduce our needs only to things that are of the greatest value to us. Additionally, it helps to rid ourselves of those things which are of less importance and less value to us. This type of life helps us to make decisions intentionally.

How to Become a Minimalist

Does minimalism help us to relieve anxiety? What actually gives birth to anxiety? Some of the things that contribute to this condition include overthinking, excessive worrying, and stressful life situations or conditions.

When you feel anxious, you also feel overwhelmed, and your mind may feel cluttered. And when your space is now clustered, filled with numerous unorganized tasks and projects, focusing on your life and relaxing becomes impossible. By definition, minimalism is a way of life that focuses on intentional decisions and designed to eliminate clutter and distractions.

An anxious life is filled with anxiety, worries, lacks focus and purpose, and delivers excessive stress. Anxiety will negatively impact your life, mood, and choices.

Attaining Anxiety Relief by Keeping Clutter to a Minimum

When you are cluttered physically, it affects your mental life. Our mental space is filled with records of belongings we have, visible or not. The organization of our space and possession is so important to a human's mental health that we dedicate time to decorate, organize, and clean at every possible opportunity. With more belongings, you are filling your life with extra tasks and decisions.

If your wardrobe is getting filled with clothes, you start to have issues deciding which clothes to wear when going out, and you waste time on making such decisions. Do you keep gifts that you don't need? You may think that getting rid of such a gift is bad, but if you never end up actually using it, it will just add to the clutter in your life.

With such clutter around you, your mind has more information to process and store. As individuals, we have different tolerance levels for clutter and cleanliness. But no one feels bad when their space is clean, clear, and organized. Try cleaning the clutter in your life, and you'll definitely find some relief from your anxiety.

How to Reduce Physical Clutters

The first step to reducing clutter is by making a list of all your belongings and going through them all. This might be a huge task, but it is worth doing. It is not a must to complete this task in a day, but make sure you build that list.

Your goal is to identify whether you love that item or not. When you're done with the list, it is best to hold on only to items that you treasure: the ones you love to own, not the ones you dislike or never use.

Use these four categories to assist you with your decluttering goals;

- Keep
- Donate
- Sell
- Discard

You can donate some of your used items to thrift stores or organizations around you that will give them to people who are really in need. You will be happy, and the receiver will also be happy. You don't need to push them all out at once, do this bit by bit, and see the joy that comes from giving.

When you clear clutter from your life, you will eliminate some stress and anxiety, and when belongings around you include only those items which bring you the greatest value, you will feel more joyful, fulfilled, and happy.

Decluttering Digitally

How to Reduce Digital Clutter

Have you ever heard of digital clutter? This type of clutter often includes your email and the files on your hard drive, or your Google drive. They can be just as overwhelming as physical clutter. When you have numerous emails to respond to, you might also feel overworked.

When you go through them and get rid of the ones that are not useful, and when you organize the ones that you need, you will feel a measure of joy and satisfaction. You don't need to address everything at once; you can just take 15 minutes out each day, week, or month to delete them bit by bit. This will result in getting rid of all your digital clutter.

You will spend a healthy amount of time to get rid of this clutter; it is not an easy job. But how do you prevent clutter from building up again? Here are some tips that will help you do this effectively; they are simple and straight to the point.

Tips to Maintain a Clutter-Free Space to Relieve Anxiety

The Number One Rule

Here is a 1-in-1-out rule you should follow. For every new item that you bring to your home, try to take one old item out. What makes up the clutter you once battle with? Clothes? Electronics? Whatever it is, always get rid of one when you buy another. You don't need to waste it; you can donate old items.

Build Space for All Items

Try to be organized. If you are organized, and you have an efficient way of storing items, they won't turn into junk. You can find shelves or boxes and keep your essentials there. But if your belongings are left in random places, even the important ones will become junk.

Ensure That Your Surfaces Are Clear

Another thing you must do is always to keep your surface clean. If you put one item on the table, it can become a natural place to keep other items. Instead of doing this, it is best to put all items in proper places in order to keep your surfaces clear. If you keep your surface clear, you easily get rid of clutter in your home.

Regularly Organize Your Paperwork

Is your clutter filled with mail and other paperwork? One thing you can do is to file your mail and paperwork in folders (digital or paper ones). Put them in places so that you can easily access them when you need to. This will help prevent important files from becoming junk.

Build an Outbox

This is not your email outbox. This should be a box or carton that should be in your garage or entrance where you keep items you will be donating or ones you will be getting rid of. If you are not sure whether you would like to give something away or not, you can keep it in this outbox. If you don't miss it while it is in the box, it is junk; get rid of the item.

Buy Intentionally

Are you struggling to get rid of the clutter in your life? One other important thing that you can do is to become intentional with the things you buy for your house. Don't just buy things because you have the money.

Always ask yourself the following question before buying anything:

- Do I need this item?
- Do I love this item?
- What do I need this item for?

If you can't find answers to any of these questions, or if you realize that you don't like the item, don't buy it. You should buy only the things you need and love. This will prevent your home and life from becoming cluttered with items that you don't use.

Do you have roommates or a romantic partner that you purchase things with? If you make purchases together, talk to them about things you will be buying and the reasons you have for wanting to buy them. You should be the one to make the final decisions about the belongings that you choose to have in your personal space, though; no one should make this decision for you.

Some people may think that a minimalist home is just a white-walled box containing furniture and no decorations. That's far from the truth. Being a minimalist does not mean you get rid of all the things you need in your life. Even if you need to stay happy and reduce overthinking by getting rid of things which others see as important, do it.

Create a healthy space for yourself: a space filled with essential things that you love to see, things that make you happy. This will reduce your anxiety dramatically.

Chapter 10

How to Make Better Decisions in Your Life

The decisions you make today do not only affect the present, they also set the tone for the future. Make better decisions today!

How often do you make decisions? Every day. No matter what we answer, though, that's the reality! We are always compelled to make decisions, though the nature of our decisions differs greatly. For example, there are big decisions and small decisions. Small decisions shouldn't take much time; big ones may take days or even weeks. And yet, we can't avoid it; we must make those decisions. However, before any decision is made, one must consider some essential factors.

Indecisiveness is a negative trait that could slow down the entire decision-making process. Most people aren't proud of the fact that they are indecisive. An indecisive person might pressure others to decide for them, either indirectly or directly.

For these people, making choices themselves can be a scary thing since they will keep asking themselves: What would eventually happen if I make a bad decision? It's normal to be fearful when you are making the decision yourself, but know that as you continue to do this, you will trust yourself more, and you will practice the act of making big decisions.

And the more you keep making significant decisions yourself, the more you will be glad to exclude other people from the decision-making process; you will need their approval less.

Therefore, since the basic idea is to make decisions yourself, independent of anyone, the following tips will help you to make decisions easily and more quickly. Consider the following six methods:

Be Aware of What You Want

One of the ways to identify what you want is to determine what your goals are. When you become more aware of what you want in life, and when you decide what your goals will be, it is evident that you will be able to make better choices. David Welch, a political science professor whose work was published in the Huffington Post, says that people who aren't self-reflective will undeniably end up making bad decisions because they aren't aware of what they want in life in the first place.

Therefore, when making a decision, you should ask yourself where you want to be next year and if that decision will help to take you where you want to go. If your answers are quite different from what you are working towards, then the best thing to do is to make a different decision. So, the critical point here is to identify what you want in life.

Ask for Advice, but Make Your Own Choices

Admittedly, making a decision doesn't mean that you should not seek advice from others; after all, no one is an island of knowledge. But you should be cautious; this could be a decision regarding your relationship, your well-being, or your job. Do you feel comfortable confiding in others and asking for their advice?

Others may not understand exactly how you feel, but should that be a reason why you shouldn't seek advice? No! You can gather information from them and make your final decision yourself. It is also important to remember that you are ultimately the one who will have to live with your decision.

Pay Attention to Your Gut

Yes, we all know ourselves better than we realize. But in some cases, most people ignore the message that their gut is telling them since they don't want to hear the consequences their decision will bring or deal with the reality of it. It is essential to be objective and clear-headed each time we are faced with some difficult choices, such as making big decisions.

Therefore, when you are making a tough decision, it's ideal to write down everything you are thinking and the reason you think you are feeling that way. As you begin to have an internal dialogue with yourself, you may become lost in an endless maze of thoughts. By writing down your thoughts, you will strengthen your conviction and are more likely to listen to your gut.

Ensure That You Are in the Right State of Mind

A person who isn't in a good mood will find it tougher to make the right decision. Unpleasant feelings that could influence the decision-making process include stress, hunger, and drowsiness.

Take, for instance, if you are trying to figure out what you will eat for lunch when you are hungry, how easily will you be able to decide? And this is a relatively small decision.

Therefore, to avoid being rash, when making a big decision, you should ensure that you are feeling comfortable and emotionally balanced. Then, after these criteria have been met, make your decision.

Learn to Trust Yourself

Don't confuse trusting yourself with arrogance and having a big ego. Experts have said that the first person an individual has to trust is himself/herself. Just because you believe in yourself doesn't make you arrogant and proud.

No one could be as consistently supportive of you in the same way that you will learn to be. Then how do you accomplish trusting yourself? Be kind to yourself; when you do, it boosts your self-confidence, and you will not need to seek approval from other people before you make any decision.

Trusting yourself, too, will let you make a sound decision eventually, even after meeting people for advice. Also, when you love and care for yourself, your connection with others becomes strengthened. Don't forget that it's a task to have the strength to trust yourself. So, as soon as confidence is met, then you will be pushed and thus be courageous to make big decisions in the future.

Practice, Practice, Practice

The way you get improve is by making your own decisions every day. If it becomes part of your day-to-day routine, you will have more confidence in decision-making and taking inspired action will get easier and faster.

According to psychologists, mastering the process of making the right decisions is depends on a lot of factors. They include a person's developmental age or stage, their idea of what's right and wrong, and their understanding of what the decision-making process entails.

Since you are unfamiliar with making big decisions for yourself, try it for a week, and don't ask anyone else to make your decisions for you. As you gradually improve, then it will become part of you, and thus you will be in control, without the influence of another person.

With these six tips, what's the bottom line? To be good at making big decisions, you really must devote a lot of time and practice. And the moment you are there, you are your own boss.

How to Stop Expecting the Worst

Have you ever thought about what keeps our brain from behaving logically? It's fear! Why? It's because fear looks so real and essential that if we dare ignore it, something terrible might happen. And that's exactly the scenario that occurs when you are expecting the worst. You are trying all you can, but it's just resulting in a magnification of your fear, anxiety, and stress.

Here is an anecdote that will explain this phenomenon further. One man said: Generally, he usually looks at his rearview mirror many times before he gets home. He knows that it's not the best thing to do, but he said he thinks doing that is the best way to be conscious and know if someone is tailgating him, and he mentions that it annoys him to see people following him.

So, one night, as he was driving home, he notices that a car is following him closely; the vehicle keeps in close contact with him, following in him every direction he goes. And after making a few turns, he started to get suspicious and asked himself: Is this person following him? Was he seen entering his car? Could they be a serial killer? Is he their next victim? Many questions were flowing, but he couldn't answer them. Maybe he's watched too many true crime shows?

He convinced himself to think positively and think of ways that he could resolve his situation. He could drive past his house so that he could fool them to disallow them from knowing where he resides. To him, it seemed like a good plan. Then something happened next.

After his next turn, he noticed that they went in a different direction; he kept going, and nothing showed up. At that time, he realized that they weren't following him anymore. What did he do next? He breathed a sigh of relief, and now he felt that it was ridiculous for him to think that they were following him.

In the real sense, that is what happens when you are anticipating or expecting the worst. At that stage, your body starts to panic; you breathe faster, your heartbeat quickens, and you start to breathe more shallowly. You will start to picture horrific scenarios in your head and alter your behavior as a result of that fear.

What happens to you during this period will affect your mood and stress level, and negatively impact your ability to make good decisions. So, how do you stop expecting the worst? Let's expand on these four points sequentially.

1. *Identify Your Fears*

First, you have to ask yourself: When you are always expecting the worst? Are those times when you deliver a presentation at work, when you are writing an exam, when you are keenly worried about your loved one's safety or your own, or when you are participating in social interactions? Yes, there are many things that could make you be fearful; identify them.

When you determine some specific scenarios, then you will have a higher tendency to identify where your fears lie and what your beliefs are about certain situations. The more you can be aware of what triggers your anxiety, thus making you expect the worst, the more that you will have the strength and power to stop it. So, don't hesitate to take a moment to reflect on when you are usually expecting the worst and why you are doing so.

If you have generalized anxiety, it's likely you expect the worst-case scenario. In that case, you are always anxious, overwhelmed, and stressed, and your heightened arousal will affect your thinking; you are more likely to overestimate adverse outcomes. Here are a few questions to ponder:

Reflection Questions:

- When do I expect the worst?
- How do these affect my emotions, thoughts, behaviors?

2. Challenge Your Expectations

Of course, when you expect the worst, your mind will always tend to create unreasonable and unrealistic scenarios. Honestly, we're blessed with the ability to imagine; it inspires wonder and creativity. The downside is that when we expect the worst, we don't always consider the facts of the situation and relative probabilities of all possible outcomes.

So, when imagining an adverse event, our fear could become so all-consuming that we will neglect the facts and fail to look at the reality. This is normal, though. But we mustn't forget that this comes from our basic need and desire for survival. To preserve our own safety, we are inclined to overestimate the tendency that bad things will happen.

Take, for example, many people who are afraid of flying. When I flew on an airplane recently, we had some turbulence, and a woman who was sitting next to me was nervous and held onto the chair that was in front of her due to fear. Like her, many other people were worried. And it's understandable; whatever happens in an airplane is definitely not in your locus of control.

However, the odds of dying in a plane crash are 1 in 11 million. You are far more likely to be either hit by lighting or be severely attacked by a shark than you will die in a plane crash. How does that make you feel? So, these facts could correctly be used to challenge the logic behind your fear.

3. Get Your Feelings Out

Emotions and thoughts can be so toxic if you have no outlet. Therefore, it is very advisable to journal and use other artistic methods to process your emotions in the right way, and that will help you to feel better.

So, write down your thoughts in a journal so you can speed up your recovery. Don't keep anything inside just because you would feel embarrassed if someone else were to read it. Also, you may speak with a trusted confidant if you would feel more comfortable doing so.

4. Take Control

To take control, you need to begin with what you have control over. As difficult as it may be to do so, it is important to let the rest go. When you sit and ponder the worst-case scenario, you are not helping yourself. So pay attention only to things you can do.

There are lots of things that you can't control; a list will assist you in clarifying them in more detail. Here are two important ones:

- What other people feel, do, or think about you.
- Situations that you have no control over.

Thus, when you focus on what you can do, you will boost your confidence level, and there will also be a decrease in your stress level; you will be able to take confident action when and where it is necessary, without overthinking.

The following four points highlight some of the best reasons why you should be able to stop expecting the worst-case scenario.

Worrying Does Not Solve Problems

Worrying does not provide you with any benefits, nor does it solve any of your problems. Don't fool yourself by thinking that the more you worry about a situation, the more you will work toward achieving it.

When you do, you are only making yourself unnecessarily stressed, tense, and anxious, which negatively will impact your ability to think critically. Therefore, each time you think about the worst-case scenario, ask yourself: Is this really helping me? It does not, and this is the first important step to mastering your thoughts, reducing your overthinking and anxiety, and improving your life.

Bonus

Overthinking Checklist

Overthinking creates problems that weren't there initially.

☐ **Broaden your perspective.**

Ask yourself: Will this matter in the next five years? Will it count in the next five weeks? Asking yourself these simple questions will help you to swiftly snap out of the overthinking zone, enabling you to pay more attention, energy, and time to what matters: things that are productive and beneficial.

☐ **Set short deadlines for decisions.**

For small decisions like washing plates or going out for a workout, spend less than 30 seconds to make your decision. For more significant decisions that would, in the past, have taken you more than a day or a few weeks for you to think through, set a deadline of about 30 minutes to think about it, or you think about it in the evening after work.

❏ Don't set yourself up for failure every day.

Read something uplifting, exercise, and then begin your most important task. This will set the right tone for the day. Focusing on one task at a time and taking breaks regularly will help you to narrow down your focus, and then you will be able to think clearly and decisively. Also, minimize your daily input like excessive email checking, which will reduce mind clutter.

❏ Become a person of action.

When you take small steps forward, one small step at a time, then you are always working towards improvement. You won't become overwhelmed, and this will stop you from plunging into procrastination.

❏ Understand that you can't control everything.

If you are trying to think things through many times, you are forcing yourself to control everything; you are trying to avoid making a mistake or experiencing failure in life. But surely those things are a part of life. They keep you out of your comfort zone. For personal growth, setbacks are essential.

☐ Say stop if you find it hard to think straight.

At times when you lie on the bed and want to take a nap, you might be occupied or filled with negative thoughts. But say to yourself: No! I'm not going to think about this now; I will choose another time. You could, for example, sleep on it.

☐ Don't get swept away by vague fears.

It's best to ask oneself, what is the worst thing that could happen? And when you have figured that out, then spend a little time to think about what could be done if that unlikely scenario happens. The fact is, the worst thing that could happen isn't usually as scary as the mind portrays it.

☐ Go to the gym and work out.

When you work out, you are becoming healthier and happier. This will make your fears disappear, and exercise will make you feel more focused and decisive.

☐ Get enough quality sleep.

164

Quality sleep is often neglected when it comes to keeping a positive mindset. Make this your favorite tip. Keep your earplugs nearby. Don't force yourself to sleep. Wind down for an extra twenty to thirty minutes on the couch. You could do this by reading, taking a warm bath, or any other activity that will gently prepare you for sleep.

☐ Reconnect with the present moment.

Slow down and reconnect with the present moment. Focus on whatever you are doing. Move slower; talk slower. Try to block out all distractions. If you are overthinking, then try to disrupt those thoughts by telling your mind: Stop! Then quickly take the next one to two minutes to focus back on the present moment. Take it in with all your senses.

☐ Spend quality time with other people who are not overthinkers.

Can you identify and recognize any sources in your life that make you overthink things? Are there people around you who think less and could be a positive influence on you? Find these people and spend time with them. Hanging around with people who have a positive impact on you will help you keep your overthinking habit at bay; in time, you will be more like them.

☐ Be aware of the issue.

You must become aware of the issue to break the habit of overthinking. But if you think that remembering this will be enough to stop you from overthinking, then you are only fooling yourself. So set a reminder, either on your phone or somewhere on your desk, that will help you realize the issue very well.

☐ Talk through your situation with a friend.

Be sure to talk to someone about the situation you are thinking about. When you vent for five minutes to a friend or trusted confidant, and he/she genuinely listens, he/she will help you to figure out the best solutions to your problems, and they will give you helpful ideas.

☐ Breathe.

Discharge the stress and calm your mind and body by entirely focusing on your breathing. Be sure to breathe in and out from your belly for just two minutes and pay attention only to the air that you are breathing in and out.

Conclusion

Worrying preoccupies your mind but does not get you anywhere!

What a gem you've unearthed! Isn't it appealing to read comprehensively about the subject of overthinking? I'm glad to provide you with an abundance of information and resources that will help you to resolve this complex issue.

Do you remember the question that I asked at the introductory part of this book? Are you closer to answering the question: Is overthinking bad for me? I'm sure that you now know the right answer. But overall, what have you learned about overthinking? First, let's review what you've read.

The first part of this book helped you to understand the principles of overthinking. The next phase assisted you to consult the bigger picture and see where you belong. Are you an overthinker or not?

The third chapter provides detailed information about how you can stop being an overthinker. You read about positive and negative thoughts and how they have, for so long, dominated many individuals. You learned how to break free from overthinking. The fifth chapter provided you with some essential ways to embrace good energy.

Furthermore, you've seen that it's possible to cope with worry, and you've been able to see ways in which you can quit worrying efficiently. In the next section, you learned practical training strategies to assist you in reducing stress and curbing anxiety.

Toward the final part of the book, you read extensively about embracing mindfulness, which was identified as one of the most efficient ways to help you get rid of overthinking. In completing this section, you've identified practical ways to relieve anxiety.

Finally, the tenth chapter gives you quality ways to make better decisions in your life. And you have seen that it's one of the ways to get rid of overthinking because when you make the right decisions, you are distracting yourself from negative thoughts, and then you will intelligently master productive thinking.

So, back to the earlier question: what have you learned? Assuredly, all the information in this book would have helped you to stop worrying, assisted you in reducing your anxiety, helped you to discard and eliminate negative thinking, and helped you to master your thoughts and make significant decisions in your life.

What should you do? You should apply the lessons that you learned in this book! That's how you will get the best from this book and earn good rewards.

To complete your task, design a working strategy for applying what you've read. You can share what you've gained from this book to teach others, such as, most importantly, your family members.

As you've agreed to devote yourself to a life that is free from overthinking, I wish you a happier life. Keep living in line with these practical and vital tips for achieving constant growth in joy in your life.

I wish you all the best!

Printed by Amazon Italia Logistica S.r.l.
Torrazza Piemonte (TO), Italy

10642549R00100